MARCO  POLO

LIS BON

ATLANTIC
OCEAN
FRANCE
PORTUGAL
ANDORRA
Lisbon
Madrid
Barcelona
SPAIN
Mallorca
Málaga
Balearics
(E)
Mediterranean
MOROCCO

T0158234

www.marco-polo.com

THE TOURING APP

shows you the way...
including routes and offline maps!

FREE!

GET MORE OUT OF YOUR MARCO POLO GUIDE

IT'S AS SIMPLE AS THIS

1 go.marco-polo.com/lis

2 download and discover

GO!

WORKS OFFLINE!

SYMBOLS

 Insider Tip

★ Highlight

⬤⬤⬤⬤ Best of...

☼ Scenic view

PRICE CATEGORIES HOTELS

Expensive over 130 euros

Moderate 80–130 euros

Budget under 80 euros

Prices are for a double room with breakfast in high season

PRICE CATEGORIES RESTAURANTS

Expensive over 30 euros

Moderate 20–30 euros

Budget under 20 euros

Prices are for a three-course meal without wine

CONTENTS

DID YOU KNOW?
Time to chill → p. 24
Spotlight on sports → p. 34
For bookworms & film buffs → p. 38
Fit in the City → p. 55
Favourite Eateries → p. 60
Local specialities → p. 62
More than a good night's sleep → p. 86
National holidays → p. 105
Currency converter → p. 109
Budgeting → p. 111
Weather → p. 112

MAPS IN THE GUIDEBOOK
(120 A1) Page numbers and coordinates refer to the street atlas and the overview map of Lisbon and surroundings on p. 138/139
(0) Site/address located off the map. Coordinates are also given for places that are not marked in the city atlas

(𝒪 A–B 2–3) refers to the removable pull-out map

INSIDE FRONT COVER:
The best Highlights

INSIDE BACK COVER:
Public transport network map

The best MARCO POLO Insider Tips

Our top 15 Insider Tips

INSIDER TIP On the hop: Lisbon's beer culture

LX Brewery is a young and dynamic team of brewers with a passion for craft beer – take a look behind this exploding scene! → **p. 76**

INSIDER TIP "Ai, Mourariiiia!"

The city's old Moorish quarter is the cradle of fado music and exhibits a street gallery of photos to commemorate its local stars. The Portuguese and English texts recount the stories behind the portraits → **p. 106**

INSIDER TIP Family Fado

Fado is everwhere in Lisbon (photo above). *A Nini* still has an authentic family ambience, especially at the regular Thursday night fado meetings → **p. 79**

INSIDER TIP Bargain hunting app

Browse through all the latest bargains to be had near you with the *Mygon* mobile app; Smartphone haters hunt down all the best discounts on the website → **p. 107**

INSIDER TIP Gastronomic whirlwind tour

Take in the culinary and other sightseeing delights of Lisbon on one of the sumptuous food tours organised by *Taste of Lisboa* → **p. 58**

INSIDER TIP Morna instead of fado

The Portuguese have fado, the inhabitants of the Cape Verde islands have morna. A lunch dance organised by the Cape Verdean association *Associação Cabo-Verdeana* will burn off the calories you have piled on from the specialities of this former Portuguese colony! → **p. 63**

INSIDER TIP Independent cultural centre

Once a hotspot for social problems, *Largo do Intendente* has now been transformed into a cool destination: it is home to cafés, the hidden-away nightlife hotspot Casa Independente, art and one of the most photogenic façades in Lisbon → **p. 76**

INSIDER TIP Secret spot

Unknown even to many locals, this hip *Teatro da Garagem (Taborda)* at the foot of the hill is the ideal location for a drink before or after a meal out in Mouraria → **p. 77**

INSIDER TIP Set sail!

Open sailing trips on the Tagus river on an historic sailing ship → **p. 109**

INSIDER TIP Bird's eye view

With a direct view of Lisbon's Elevador de Santa Justa and affordable meals, the *café-restaurant* has transformed the top-floor of the *kitchenware store Pollux* → **p. 93**

INSIDER TIP Hiking through the fairy forest

Only the seven dwarves are missing. Hike through the enchanted forests and parks around picturesque *Sintra* (photo below) a short train ride from Lisbon → **p. 55**

INSIDER TIP World-class panorama

Enjoy the view from the terrace of the windmill-turned-bar *Moinho Dom Quixote* suspended above the rocky coast near Cabo da Roca → **p. 55**

INSIDER TIP Urban development up close

Take an inspiring sightseeing tour (and a snack) through the popular Mouraria quarter organised by the friendly and enthusiastic neighbourhood association *Mouradia!* → **p. 80**

INSIDER TIP Fado – the real thing

Are you looking for that authentic fado atmosphere away from touristy performances? Then book a ticket for a *Fado Night Tour* with evening meal included → **p. 79**

INSIDER TIP Creative containers

Village Underground offers hand-roasted coffee, snacks and clubbing events built around shipping containers and double-decker buses → **p. 80**

BEST OF...

GREAT PLACES FOR FREE
Discover new places and save money

FOR FREE

● *Greenery, scenery...*
Lisbon has no shortage of pretty and freely accessible beauty spots. The labyrinthine garden of the *Museu Calouste Gulbenkian* is a favourite with couples for *namorar* (romantic assignments), for impromptu picnics and to while away the hours reading or smoking (photo) → p. 51

● *Free city tour*
The lively group of *Wild Walkers* offer amusing guided tours with varying routes and themes (pub crawl, fado evening) through their city. Since most tours are for free, we strongly recommend a generous tip for this young, wild crew of enthusiastic guides → p. 110

● *Collector items in cultural centre*
Admission to the *Joe Berardo's collection of contemporary art* in the *Centro Cultural de Belém* is zero as is the walk along the riverfront to Lisbon's new star museum *MAAT* → p. 79

● *Sacred view*
With no restaurant or bar on the *Miradouro Senhora do Monte,* simply buy yourself a cool beer from the shop down on Calçada da Graça to take in this panoramic view. If the chapel is open, offer the sexton a tip to show you the throne of São Gens where generations of pregnant women have sat in the hope of an easy childbirth → p. 32

● *A march through history*
For those who enjoy walking, the 14 km/8.7 miles *biodiversity route* from Belém to Monsanto takes you to locations of scientific and historical interest → p. 53

● *Free art at the Ritz*
Learn more about some of the biggest names in *contemporary Portuguese art,* in particular Almada Negreiros, in luxurious surroundings at the Ritz → p. 36

(●●●●) Dots in guidebook refer to "Best of..." tips

● *Terraces with a view*

Lisboetas, like tourists, are forever hunting the best view of the city and Tagus river. One of the finest vantage points is the *Miradouro São Pedro de Alcântara* looking across to the Old Town and Castelo → p. 41

● *Coffee culture*

Students and office workers, elderly ladies and Atlantic coast surfers: they all share one habit – stopping for a coffee at any opportunity. The most famous and atmospheric place for this is the *Café A Brasileira* in Chiado (photo) → p. 59

● *Happy to be sad*

You'll hear fado, the "Portuguese blues", with its undertones of melancholy and longing, on every corner in Lisbon. Don't miss a live performance in one of the atmospheric fado venues → p. 21, 79

● *A Streetcar named Nostalgia*

The old-fashioned yellow trams are used by tourists and locals alike. The famous No. 28 offers the best ride in town, rumbling up and down through narrow alleys, inches from the houses → p. 26

● *Stay on the ball*

Everybody knows that the people who brought us Figo and Ronaldo are football-mad. At the local derby between Benfica and Sporting things get pretty heated. But even "regular" league games are always worth a party → p. 34

● *Look down*

Lisbon's famous *calçada,* pavements laid by skilled craftsmen, occasionally take on fabulous shapes and forms. Cast your eyes over the wave patterns on *Rossio square* or the phallic representations between the Brasileira café and the Benetton store in Chiado → p. 39

● *Up the town and down the town*

One of Lisbon's icons are the *elevadores,* funiculars and lifts that have been transporting people up to Chiado and the Bairro Alto for over 100 years. Don't miss being whizzed down in the cast-iron tower of the *Elevador de Santa Justa*! → p. 35

ONLY IN

BEST OF...

AND IF IT RAINS
Activities to brighten your day

● *Sea creatures*
At the *Oceanarium,* one of the largest in Europe, wet afternoons pass quickly among the sharks, marine turtles and sun fish → p. 103

● *Coach Museum*
With its splendid historic coaches, the *Museu Nacional dos Coches* in Belém is the most popular museum in Lisbon, now in its ambitious "hovering" new home → p. 48

● *Culinary paradise under cover*
Take a whirlwind tour of Lisbon's food trends by strolling through the market hall of *Time Out Mercado da Ribeira* which sells gourmet hamburgers, wok cuisine, sushi, the world's best chocolate cake... → p. 71

● *Temple of books*
Fábula Úrbis is arguably the best bookshop in town, and a great place for book-lovers to while away a rainy hour or two. Pick up a coffee from upstairs and browse its excellent selection of English-language titles → p. 68

● *Shopping in style*
Join those Lisboetas who refuse to let precarious finances ruin their love of shopping, *ir as compras.* Enjoy the shops and people-watching below the postmodern towers of *Amoreiras* or in the mega *Centro Comercial Colombo* → p. 68

● *A factory of hip culture and ideas*
Today, it's ideas rather than textiles that are produced at *LX Factory.* Among other locations, it houses restaurants, a cool bookshop (photo), a space for experimental music, designer shops, the popular Rio Maravilha Bar and clubs → p. 80

RAIN

RELAX AND CHILL OUT
Take it easy and spoil yourself

● *Pole position*
Many trendy terrace cafés such as the *Esplanada das Portas do Sol* often have comfy sofas on which to chill out. And they offer their guests fantastic views over the city → **p. 32**

● *Float away*
Let the saline solution in the floating tank at *Float In* carry you into a state of complete relaxation – you can't be more relaxed than this!
→ **p. 24**

● *Experience Belém in peace and quiet*
The *Mosteiro dos Jerónimos* in Belém draws the tourists like bees to a honeypot. Come early, shortly before 10am, to catch the magical peace of the cloisters without the crowds → **p. 46**

● *Kick back on the beach*
Even in spring or autumn it is usually warm enough to sit by the sea, or even take a dip. Don't worry about a picnic hamper, just sit yourself down in one of the many beach cafés lining the *Costa Caparica* → **p. 53**

● *Go with the flow*
Board a Tagus ferry or a river cruising boat and lean back, enjoying the laid-back atmosphere on board and the wonderful views of the city from the water → **p. 27, 110**

● *Palace garden*
Spoil yourself with a massage and other spa treatments in the *Garden Spa* of the *Pestana Palace Hotel*, overlooking the splendid gardens of a 19th-century palace → **p. 24**

● *Uplifting reading*
Grab your holiday reading and climb up to the *Castelo de São Jorge* (photo). Afterwards, find a quiet spot in this extensive complex to read your book and soak up the fabulous city views – sheer balm for the soul! → **p. 29**

INTRODUCTION

DISCOVER LISBON!

Lisbon is the place to be and be seen. Tourism is booming in the city. The Portuguese capital is experiencing a shower of prizes from "Europe's best city destination" to "Europe's best cruise port" ...a gold-rush mood is gripping Lisbon. In 2016, it was named as the new host city of the Web Summit which attracts 40,000 IT professionals each year. Pop legend Madonna has also put up camp with her family here. Lisbon is a darling on Instagram. It is no coincidence that the city is a favourite hang-out for *photographers and artists* who love the contrasts between the traditional and modern, its morbid charm and its *special light*. Lisbon's trademark seven hills encompass the city like an amphitheatre and the chalky white *calçada-portuguesa* mosaic pavements reflect the dazzling sunlight. *Colours dominate the cityscape*: the deep blue of the sky above the dazzling white churches, the sunlight yellow of the trams and buses, the inviting bright red of the rooftop tiles, the lilac cloud of the Jacarandá trees in bloom and last but not least the glistening silver Tagus River which runs through it. If there's one golden rule when visiting Lisbon, it's never forget your camera!

Lisbon also holds the title as the *sunshine capital* of Europe. It has the sunniest days in all of Western Europe with an average 3300 sunny hours a year. With a Mediter-

Photo: View of the old city with the statue of King Pedro IV on the Rossio

ranean climate, Lisbon also enjoys a cool Atlantic breeze which takes the edge of the summer highs making the city bearable even in high summer. Even though the city centre lies approx. 12 kilometres away from the seafront, the Tagus River provides the perfect holiday setting and, if the mood takes you, you can stroll along the riverfront which stretches from the Praça do Comércio to Belém. Despite its attractions, the city remains *affordable*. Although prices have risen over the last few years, you can still eat extremely well for little money, with lunchtime menus for just 10 euros. Cheap accommodation is also availa-

> **With a cool Atlantic breeze: holiday mood along the Tagus**

ble in a city rated as one of the world's best hostel locations. At the same time, Lisbon is an amiable and friendly city. *Só um bocadinho – just a moment, please* – is the polite response of busy waiters and sellers to guests in a hurry. For a city that has experienced so many trials and tribulations over the years, its residents remain laid-back...

And the city has certainly witnessed a turbulent past: The Phoenicians were the first to settle here and establish a trading post. Later, the Carthaginians, Indo-European Celts, Romans, Germanic tribes, Moors, Brazilians and Southeast Asians came and left their own heritage to create a city with a special identity – a city of *tolerance* which is still felt today. Five centuries of Roman rule have left its mark in this city formerly known as Olissipo with remains of stone fermentation tanks once used to salt garum, a fish sauce considered a delicatessen and shipped across the Roman Empire. When the Romans retreated at the end of the 5th century, forced away to defend their Empire on

Awe-inspiring buildings such as the Hieronymus Monastery remind you of Lisbon's world trading past

other frontiers, a vacuum of power emerged which was quickly exploited by Visigoths, Alans and Huns who all swept into the peninsula. From the start of the 8th century, the *Moors* – Arabs - invaded from the South. The city has them to thank for the mighty Castelo fortifications where the Moors, Christians and Jews once lived in Al Uxbuna.

The practice of religious tolerance came to an end in 1147 with the reconquest of the city at the hands of an army of Christian crusaders. The Moors were banished to a district along the hill east of the centre, Mouraria, for a long time a neglected neighbourhood but now the city's trendiest spot. There is no shortage of photo opportunities, be it an Easter Day procession, the Chinese New Year festival or crowds of young Indians throwing bags of coloured powder to celebrate Holi festival on the multi-cultural square, Martim Moniz. A decade ago, this square,

The city's trendiest neighbourhood is the multi-cultural Mouraria

where long queues of visitors wait to take the famous tram 28, was virtually deserted. Today, Martim Moniz is the *multicultural hotspot* of Mouraria with its gigantic Chinese dragons and food stalls. People from over 50 nations can be heard speaking dozens of different languages in the old Moorish neighbourhood and live here side by side in harmony.

This diverse mix of languages is just as much part of the city's sound track as the rattling and brrrrinnnggg of the *historic trams* or the cries of lottery-ticket sellers:

hoje anda a rooooda! (the wheel of fortune is spinning today! – by the way, it's a fact that no other European nation spends so much money on lottery tickets as the Portuguese!). The *sounds of music* are in the air in the warm summer months, with open-air concerts playing everything from fado to opera. Today, the city's cacophony is added to by the rattling of suitcase wheels along the cobbled streets dragged by the endless crowds of tourists. In contrast, the soft Portuguese language is a more pleasing sound to the ear and is easy to decipher, at least when read, if you have knowledge of other Romanic languages. Understanding spoken Portuguese is a far different matter: If you're unfamiliar to the language, the nasal tones and tongue-clicking sounds make *português* a difficult language to master.

The most historic event in the city's history took place on November 1, 1755 when an *earthquake* hit, engulfing the city in flames for days and reducing it to rubble and ash. From this chaos emerged the man-of-the-hour, Marquês de Pombal, who immediately brought order and began to rebuild the city and develop the new Baixa. Today, the district is an interesting hybrid of old and new: made-in-China souvenir shops are edging out traditional businesses which have been around for centuries while the buildings designed by Pombal have been restored to their former glory. The reasons why the city still treasures many old buildings (admittedly some are in a desolate state) can be found in history: Portugal remained neutral in World War II. The dictator Salazar remained on good terms with both parties: He supported the Allies by allowing them to set up base on the Azores islands and provided Nazi Germany with wolfram for arms production. In the 1940s, Lisbon was *Europe's last safe haven.* The German writers Hannah Arendt, Heinrich Mann and Stefan Zweig all emigrated to Lisbon and described the city of light as a symbol of hope

Carnations stuck into rifles' muzzles gave the revolution its name

in war-bombed Europe. In turn, the new inhabitants brought change to the city which was still living under the repressive regime of Salazar: women started wearing miniskirts and daring bikinis and tables were placed outside bars – something we take for granted today. Salazar died in 1970 yet Europe's longest reigning dictatorship managed to hold on longer to the reign of power. The police state was swept away on 25 April 1974 by a peaceful revolution by generals despairing of the colonial ways. This had the support of the people and was known as the *"Carnation Revolution"* – named after the red carnations *(cravos)* placed in the muzzles of soldiers' rifles.

Following the carnation revolution, the city came out of the shadows of dictatorship and saw new influences in its urban fabric: The return of Portuguese settlers in Africa who no longer had a future in the new independent republics of Angola and Mozambique. Half a million *retornados* came to Lisbon and were integrated together with immigrants from the former African colonies, Portuguese Africans, who were seeking new opportunities in their "motherland".

Football and expo: A revitalisation of the city

Joining the European Union in the mid-1980s was an important step for Portugal – and the country's capital also profited from EU funding. The city exploded to life during the 1990s; Lisbon hosted the Football European Championships in 1994. In 1998, visitors from around the world came to the capital for the *Expo World Exhibition*; industrial wasteland was transformed into a new neighbourhood which remains well integrated in the cityscape, twenty years later. The major *financial crisis* in 2008 dealt Portugal with a massive blow and the country could only be saved from state bankruptcy by an 80-million euro bailout from "Troika" (comprising the European Commission, the European Central Bank, and the International Monetary Fund). Today, the city is witnessing a building boom with investments from all sides. Europe's biggest cruise ship port stands at the foot of the Alfama district. The Portuguese are slowly working their way up the bottom of the European fertility table after registering the lowest birth rate in Europe with its overaged population. Few of Lisbon's 550,000 inhabitants (2 million in its urban area) actually live in the historic city centre due to the influx of tourists...

Tourism, well what can we say? On the one hand, the city welcomes the boom: An increasing percentage of the gross national product is generated by tourism. Rows on rows of apartments are under renovation in the streets of Alfama and Mouraria, if only for them to be rented out to tourists on sites such as Airbnb. Apartment owners are moving out of the popular historic old city streets into neighbouring districts to make room for paying guests. Locals are struggling to find affordable living space:

The pride of Lisbon: Praça do Comercio – the square of commerce

Gentrification has arrived in Lisbon too and comes with a backlash against mass tourism. Something one tour operator has picked up on, ironically calling itself *"We Hate Tourism"*. Lisbon is keen to avoid becoming a "second Barcelona", an amusement park city with few "real inhabitants" and swamped by camera-clicking tourists.

What can Lisbon expect in the next years? The city is expanding to the east. In Marvila between the inner city and the Expo site, enormous warehouses are being renovated along the Tagus to accommodate cool galleries, bars and co-working spaces behind their splendid turn-of-the-century facades. A new airport is planned on the opposite banks of the Tagus to alleviate the pressure on the city's existing airport, the Aéroporto Humberto Delgado – which was renamed in 2016 in honour of the "General without fear" who publicly opposed dictator Salazar. Lisbon has gained in confidence and has changed its tune from the *triste fado* to playing *positive sounds for the future*.

WHAT'S HOT

1 Food to go

Piaggios, vintage cars and co. The exploding "meals on wheels" scene has hit Lisbon – with fluffy focaccia bread (at the Feira-da-Ladra flea market), a bar serving a taste of Portuguese wines *(Wine With A View* in Castelo and in Belém), bagels, burgers, frozen yoghurt...the food trucks are just as diverse in style as their snacks: piaggios and vintage vans, trailers and caravans. You can even enjoy the view on the Miradouro Nossa Senhora do Monte with a homemade lemonade or *Pastel de Nata*. Information on street-food festivals is available on Facebook.

AirBnB for food

2

Visit the cook at home An exciting alternative to a restaurant: *Portuguese Table-Service (25–55 euros | www.portuguesetable.com)* invites you to dine at the home of (hobby) cooks and make new friends over a love of food. This new network likes to gather people unknown to each other around the table. You won't be disappointed as all the cooks have been tested beforehand and once you register free-of-charge you can view the ratings of your guest cook. A veteran supper club is *www.28alisbon.com (40 euros)*.

3 Call of the mountains

Cross-country adventures The Portuguese used to leave hiking – *caminhar* – to foreigners. Today, they too have discovered the delights of exploring nature on foot. Whole groups trek through the region's canyons and along beach trails. It's cheap to join (approx. 5 euros) because the groups are usually large in number. *Caminhos Com Carisma* (Facebook, since 2012), *www.greentrekker. pt* and *Caminhadas Smile* (Facebook) all take you on original hikes.

Spray and stencil

Urban art   Street art came late to Lisbon but now there's no holding it back. One favourite artist is Vhils, another is Bordalo II, a grandson of Portugal's most famous ceramic artist. Explore the streets on your own with the book "Street Art Lisbon 2" with city map. The best way though is to take a tour with the *graffiti and stencil experts from www.lisbonstreetarttours.com* who will show you the works of art. *Underdogs gallery (Rua Doutor Estévão de Vasconcelos | www.under-dogs.net)* in the trendy district of Marvila offers mini-bus tours. A particular highlight are the tours on foot (usually on the last Sat. in the month with English-language assistance on request) through the enormous open-air galleries of the socially vulnerable districts *Quinta do Mocho (Facebook: Arte Publica Loures)* and *Bairro Padre Cruz (Facebook: Boutique da Cultura)*.

Greeting the sun

Yoga   The yoga craze has spread to Lisbon and those wishing to greet the sun on their holidays have a wide choice of establishments: *Foodprintz café (Rua Rodrigo da Fonseca 82a | www.foodprintz cafe.com)* offers Hatha/ Yivamukti yoga sessions. The *MeetUp platform (www.meetup.com)* informs you of when and where the next session is to be held – whether in the park or on the rooftop. Tip: You're in the best hands with Lisbon local and certified *Hatha/ Iyengar instructor Rita Pereira (sessions available in English | pre-booking necessary | 10 euros for 75 min. | www.yogaloveyoga.weebly.com)*. SUP yoga, performed on large stand-up paddling boards, is a must for water-loving yoga fans. Available at the Bay of Cascais *(www.surfnpaddle.com)*.

IN A NUTSHELL

TYPICAL!

The pace in Lisbon is certainly slower than in other European capitals. Apart from motorists, Lisboetas will not be hurried: they will happily take a waiting ticket at the cheese counter and always have time for a chat with their neighbours. If you know the London rush hour, the Metro will appear a cosy coffee party to you. Coffee rather than tea: Lisboetas celebrate their coffee culture and take time out to spend with their friends, the *convivio*. Statistically, compared with their European counterparts, the Portuguese are among the latest to go to bed, and have the most difficulty getting up in the morning. While the Portuguese have the second-longest working hours in Europe after the British, their productivity doesn't match the hours they put in. They sometimes accuse themselves of being a self-deprecating nation of people.

A big problem: Lisbon's city centre is losing inhabitants. Couples with children soon realise how difficult it is to push a buggy up and down the steep, cobble-stoned streets. Popular alternatives are the chic avenidas or the nicer suburbs, even though the neighbourhood feel is very different there – for example, the modern *condominios,* closed communities, may not permit their occupants to hang washing outside the windows, since that ruins appearances. It's mostly young foreigners who enjoy moving into the characterful (though usually modernised) apartments of the Old Town. They are prepared to put up with tum-

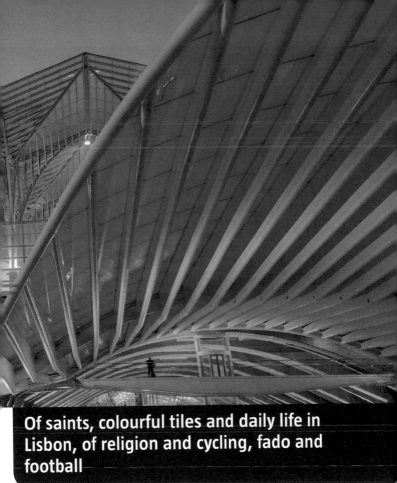

Of saints, colourful tiles and daily life in Lisbon, of religion and cycling, fado and football

bledown façades, a problematic sewage system and signs of social deprivation outside their front door in return for the charm of living in a bairro histórico.

AZULEJOS

Azulejos (pronounced: azoolay-shoosh) can bee seen everywhere in Lisbon. The colourful tiles adorn the walls of houses and benches, staircases and arches. The art of tiling is part of the city's Moorish heritage, and the name is derived from the Arabic al zu-laique ("small polished stone"). Tiled landscapes and scenes of daily life tell a lot about Portugal's history and culture. The Museu Nacional do Azulejo (see p. 51) gives an excellent overview of the history of the tiled images. A new generation of tile artists is treading new paths, choosing unusual motifs and exploring different formats.

FADO OR KIZOMBA?

● Fado is the Portuguese blues. It was born in the poor neighbourhoods of Lisbon, Alfama and Mouraria in the first half of the 19th century, and for a long time had a disreputable reputation. The word is derived from the Latin *fatum* (fate). While both men and women *(fadistas)* sing the fado, it is always accompanied by two men, usually with stoic expressions, working two string instruments, a classic guitar and a kind of lute, the *guitarra portuguesa*. In terms of subject matter, the fado revolves around love, Lisbon, hope and disappointment – and most of all the *saudade* (see below), a distinctly Portuguese feeling. What fado means to the Portuguese was evident in 1999, when Amália Rodrigues, the "Queen of Fado", died. A three-day period of state mourning was declared. To this day, nobody can compare with the goddess of fado, but there are many new names on the scene, such as Camané and the internationally successful Mariza. Young stars such as Sara Tavares, of Cape Verdean heritage, the charismatic shooting star Ana Moura and the strong-voiced Cristina Branco have breathed new life into the genre.

But you will also hear other music, too: Come in June for the celebrations honouring the patron saints and you won't be able to ignore *pimba,* accordion-supported songs with unequivocally equivocal lyrics. Lisbon's Cape Verdeans sing their heartfelt *morna* – you might know the late Cesaria Evora's successful ballad "Sodade". The Angolan community likes to dance the *kuduro,* a slighty hectic but eminently danceable sound. Portugal's internationally successful kuduro band is Buraka Som Sistema from the suburb of Amadora. The calmer *kizomba* is danced intimately entwined, and the newest trend is Afro House. Da Weasel and Boss AC are the most famous Lisbon rappers. Traditional dances are witnessing a major revival in Portugal, more information on these informal ball dances, workshops and events can be found at: *www.tradballs.pt.*

Cyclists are slowly becoming a frequent sight in the city

RIGHT OF WAY

Lisbon's cyclists are starting to stake a claim on the city streets, very gently; if you want to meet them, hire a bike on the last Friday of the month, get yourself to the central Marquês de Pombal roundabout at 6pm and join the *Massa Crítica (www.massacriticapt.net)*, where a couple of dozen Lisboetas claim the street for themselves. The whole thing is done in polite Portuguese style: one lane is left free for motorised traffic. The city authorities are slowly increasing the number of cycle paths, because the grooves of the *eléctricos* are death traps for cyclists, who also have to deal with the contempt of bus and taxi drivers. A bicycle-friendly map of the city is available online: *www.cicloviaslx.com*, bikes to hire from *Bikeiberia* (see p. 109).

THE ART OF THE FORTUNATE KING

Portugal's most influential contribution to art history was only given its name "Manueline" in the 19th century but it will forever be attributed to "King Manuel I the Fortunate" of the Golden Age (1495–1521). This style of late Gothic art, found specifically in Portugal, incorporates maritime elements and representations of the voyages of discovery such as twisted ship's ropes, anchors, palm arches, plants and animals which the discovers had found in the new world. Columns carved like twisted strands of rope direct the viewer's gaze upwards. The armillary sphere, a rudimentary navigational instrument and the personal emblem of Manuel I as well as the cross of the Order of Christ, the military order that helped to finance the first voyages of discovery, are also frequently encountered in this art form. Influences of the Spanish Plateresque movement with vines and animal figures, which is characteristic of Spanish silversmith crafts, can also be seen as well as motifs taken from the Christ's Passion; Dom Manuel liked to see himself as a saviour of the people. The best examples are the Hieronymus Monastery and in the fortress of the Belém Tower.

PATRON SAINTS

Lisbon has not one, but two patron saints. The official one is São Vicente, a Spanish martyr whose body was guided safely to Lisbon on a rudderless boat from the Cabo de São Vicente on the Algarve by a pair of ravens. However, the alfacinhas venerate their true patron saint, Santo António, much more. Born in 1195 in Lisbon, Santo António spent most of his life as a preacher and Franciscan monk in France and Italy, dying in 1231 in a monastery near Padua (elsewhere in the world he is venerated as St Antonius of Padua). The saint is credited with numerous miracles, and is the patron saint of lovers and the poor. In this tradition, every year the city finances a stylish wedding in the cathedral for poor couples. Convenient for tourists who have mislaid a charger or a credit card: Santo António is also the patron saint of the forgetful.

WHAT DO YOU BELIEVE IN?

90 per cent of the population are Roman-Catholic. On feast days, statues of saints such as Our Lady of the Pains are carried through the city in processions. One Pope declared the Portuguese to be "the most religious people in the world", and the 100th anniversary of Fátima's Marian apparition brought hundreds of thousands of visitors to Portugal in 2017. However, they don't take their religion all that seriously. The churches are not exactly crowded. The umbrella of Catholi-

cism encompasses many ancient customs and rites, forming an eclectic mix of religious belief and superstition. People vow great devotion to their favourite saint, and every problem has a patron saint who can sort it out. Santa Lúcia helps with eye complaints, São Braz with colds. In some neighbourhoods, you'll see shop windows full of votive candles to guard against the evil eye or financial ruin alongside statuettes of Nossa Senhora da Fátima. On top of that, Brazilian and Angolan immigrants have imported their own eclectic customs.

QUIRKY WRITER

Lisboetas have commemorated Fernando Pessoa (1888–1935), probably Portugal's most famous poet, with a bronze monument in front of his favourite café, *A Brasileira*. Today, few of the countless tourists who have their picture taken alongside the statue have actually read Pessoa's obsessive prose and poetry, tinged with nihilism. Pessoa's name and his work are intimately connected with the city. As witty as he was eccentric, the intellectual wrote under different names, worked as a foreign languages corre-spondence clerk in the Baixa and moved house many times within the city. During his lifetime, Pessoa, whose name means "person", published very little, but his work is currently experiencing a renaissance beyond the borders of Portugal. In the poet's last residence in Campo de Ourique, which has been converted into a small arts centre with a library, fans can follow in the footsteps of this genius of modernism: the *Casa Fernando Pessoa (Mon–Sat 10am–6pm, English-language guided tours Mon, Fri, often Sat 11.30am | admission 4 euros | Rua Coelho da Rocha 16 | casafernandopessoa.cm-lisboa.pt | eléctrico 25, 28 Rua Saraiva Carvalho)*. Still worth reading: Pessoa's poetic city guide written in 1930, *Lisbon – what the Tourist Should See,* also available on DVD.

SAUDADE

"Like a dagger working in the heart" is how the Portuguese will sometimes explain the feeling of sheer boundless melancholy known as *saudade* – a word that cannot be translated as sorrow, fatalism, sentimentalism, nostalgia or melancholy, as it combines a little bit of all of them. The roots of this passionate feeling are

TIME TO CHILL

The uncrowned queen among Lisbon's spas is the ● *Garden Spa* **(132 A4)** *(M F10) (Rua Jau 54 | tel. 2 13 61 56 00 | www.pestana.com | best take a taxi)*at the *Pestana Palace Hotel*. You'll be spoilt for choice in this 19th-century palace turned hotel: enjoy a caviar facial, a chocolate body pack, a hot stone treatment or a relaxing Ayurveda massage. A fabulous view of the gardens surround-ing the palace is included – giving the eyes a treat, too. For complete relaxation, take an hour in the saline solution of the ● *Float In* floating tank **(134 A2)** *(M K8) (Rua San Filipe Nery 37A | tel. 2 13 88 01 93 | 9 15 78 58 21 | www.float-in.pt | metro (yellow) Rato)*. The brain switches off completely, and the leg muscles can unwind from a day spent pounding the city streets *(50 min. from 45 euros)*.

considered to lie in the Islamic era, and it finds its artistic expression in the famous fado music. In conversation with Lisbon's older generation, you'll often find a general fatalism at work. When asked how things are going, they will often reply, "Eh, cá estou" (well, here I am) or "Vai-se andando" (things are going), comparable perhaps to the English expression "mustn't grumble". This fatalistic attitude combined with a rigid hierarchical social structure often produces a kind of lethargy when applied to economy and finances which can clash with the dynamic and efficient character of northern European tourists.

FOOTBALL AS A RELIGION

Gooooooooool! Goooooaaaal! Portugal is home to the reigning European football champions and if you happen to pick up on a conversation about football in one of the city's tascas, you'll surely hear the names of "Ben-feeee-kah" and Sporting dropped in. Lisbon's two football teams are hot topics in the city's cafés and tavernas, particular when the trainer, Jorge Jesus, decides to swap from one club to the other – scandal! You are defined by the football club you follow. When Benfica won the championship two years in succession, a Benfica shirt was flown in by crane for the statue of Marquês de Pombal to wear. And the only newspaper to still be printed in the former press district of Bairro Alto is called "A Bola" – the ball.

ANTÓNIO & MARCELO

Two Portuguese politicians are worth knowing: António Costa and Marcelo Rebelo de Sousa. The residing Prime Minister, António Costa, belonging to the PS (socialist party) is known as "the Samosa from Mouraria" by his political

Benfica's stadium – sporting ground or pilgrim site?

opponents due to his Indian heritage. In his term as Mayor of Lisbon, he invested a lot of energy into the revitalisation of this run-down Moorish quarter. The charismatic lawyer, television commentator and strict Catholic "Marcelo" is the current President of Portugal and expresses his opinions on all possible issues despite his representative position. His favourite subject is the fight against homelessness and he is sometimes seen selling the magazine for the homeless. He is head of a minority government based on a confidence-and-supply agreement with two left-wing, known as *geringonça*. Even the French President Emmanuel Macron has visited Lisbon to find out more about how this works.

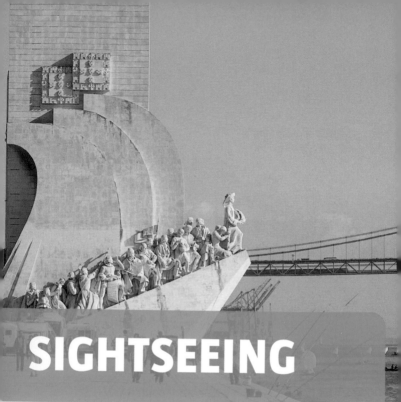

SIGHTSEEING

CITY **WHERE TO START?**
Rossio **(120 B–C2)** *(∅ M9)*:
From Rossio, officially Praça Dom Pedro IV, either reach the banks of the Tagus in a 10-min walk through the Baixa or head up the hill to the Castelo de São Jorge (approx. 15 minutes thanks to the Elevador do Castelo from Rua Fanqueiros). Or take Rua do Carmo in the direction of Chiado for shopping and museums. To get to the party zone of Bairro Alto from Rossio, head for the Restauradores square and take the Elevador da Glória funicular from there. The Metro station is Rossio (green); many buses pass the square, including the airport service.

While Lisbon has no shortage of grand monuments, it's most of all the small things that make the city on the Tagus what it is. The best way to explore and experience the capital is on foot.

Stroll across magnificent squares, lose yourself in the maze of alleyways, and enjoy fantastic views from the many *miradouros* (viewpoints) of the city built on seven hills. Join the Lisboetas in one of the many Lisbon cafés for a *bica* (espresso) or a *galão* (milky coffee). Or board one of the ancient trams. These splendid, old-fashioned trams have been trundling through the narrow streets of the city centre for over 100 years. Many of the old lines are no longer running. A ride on the ★ ● *Eléctrico 28* is one of the best and cheapest tours of Lisbon, as

A ride on the funicular or a stroll through narrow alleyways – it's the little pleasures that make Lisbon a big adventure

it trundles through the entire city centre. On public transport maps, it is marked with an E like all Eléctricos. In order to get a seat, especially if you're with a group of people, it's best to board at the beginning of the run at Martim Moniz. Without wanting to dampen the holiday spirit: do watch your wallet!

In the light of the setting sun, Lisbon shows off its classic beauty. The best vantage point for catching this mood is the river. Just board one of the many ● Tagus ferries, and take a little detour to the other side of the river, from central Cais do Sodré to Cacilhas for instance. Close to the ferry port you'll find a couple of attractive terrace restaurants on the river. **INSIDER TIP** Don't be deterred by the crumbling state of the harbour promenade and keep on walking to the right to catch that authentic Lisbon feeling!

The national museums of the capital are dedicated to the glorious past of Portugal. The themes revolve around the exciting time of the Discoveries, Portugal's empire and the Golden Age. Exotic treas-

DISTRICT MAP

BAIXA & AVENIDA
PAGE → 33

CAMPO DE OURIQUE, LAPA & MADRAGOA
PAGE → 42

ALFAMA, MOURARIA & GRAÇA
PAGE → 28

BELÉM, RESTELO & AJUDA
PAGE → 44

CHIADO & BAIRRO ALTO
PAGE → 39

The map shows the location of the most interesting districts. There is a detailed map of each district on which each of the sights described is numbered.

ures from foreign lands are a reminder of the past glories of this small country. Many Lisbon museums are housed in palaces that used to belong to the nobility, making them worth seeing for this reason alone. Even if you can't bear museums, be aware that INSIDER TIP some of the most beautiful terrace cafés belong to museums, the one of the Museu Nacional de Arte Antiga among them.

With the old-fashioned *elevadores* (lifts) you can make short work of some of Lisbon's hills, in style. They include three nostalgic, electric funiculars. All of these curious means of transport are over 100 years old. A return transport ticket costs 3.60 and 5 euros; you're much better off buying an all-day ticket (6.15 euros) for Metro and Carris (the company that runs the buses and *elevadores*).

ALFAMA, MOURARIA & GRAÇA

Old Lisbon clusters around the Castelo de São Jorge, with the historic neighbourhoods of Alfama and Mouraria nestling below.

The former Moorish settlement of Alfama is Lisbon's oldest neighbourhood. Miraculously, the quarter survived the devastating earthquake of 1755 virtually unscathed, and its medieval character has been preserved. This bairro histórico is a modest working-class area characterised by a maze of steep, narrow stairs, tiny lanes and leafy squares. Similarly labyrinthine, more derelict, yet very trendy today, is neighbouring Mouraria. This is where the Moors were banished after the Christian reconquest of the city in 1147. In June, Alfama celebrates its patron saint, Santo António, with street parties, music and dance. Adjoining Alfama, to the northeast, is Graça, a vibrant 19th-century residential quarter. Graça has several magnificent buildings, including the monastery church of *São Vicente de Fora*, historical workers' quarters such as the *Vila Berta* (135 E3) (*M O8*), some viewpoints and the *Feira da Ladra* flea market (see p. 70) twice a week.

1 CASA DOS BICOS (121 E4) (*M N10*)

The *House of Spikes*, a city palace built in Italian style in 1523, owes its name to its façade of pointy stonework. Today, the *Fundação José Saramago (Tue–Sat 10am–6pm, guided tours about life and work Wed 3.30pm, Fri 11.30am | admission 3 euros, guided tour 4 euros | www.josesaramago.org)* of the Nobel-Prize winning author José Saramago who died in 2010 has its headquarters here.

Saramago's ashes were buried in front of the building. INSIDER TIP Visiting the interesting archaeological excavations in the basement is free! *Rua dos Bacalhoeiros 9–11 | metro (blue) Terreiro do Paço*

2 CASTELO DE SÃO JORGE ★ ≋ (121 D–E2) (*M N9*)

The castle dedicated to St George is the cradle of Lisbon. Impossible to miss, it occupies a prominent position above the rooftops of the city. The steep climb up the castle hill is rewarded by amazing views. ● You can recuperate from your exertions on the stone benches under shady trees. This medieval citadel was a base for many of the country's rulers. Founded in the fifth century by the Visigoths, later on, the fort was taken and extended by the Moors. In 1147, King Dom Afonso Henriques and his followers recaptured the castle. Turned into a royal residence, in the early 16th century, the Portuguese royal family (King Manuel I) moved out down to the river, and the castle fell into disrepair. To mark the 800th anniversary of the *Reconquista* (reconquest), the fort and its defensive

---

MARCO POLO HIGHLIGHTS

Today, the Igreja de Santa Engrácia serves as Portugal's national pantheon

towers were reconstructed in 1938. An exhibition documents the way of life and customs of the former inhabitants.

On the *Ulisses* Tower, the periscope of the *Câmara Escura* (camera obscura) projects a 360-degree panorama of the city onto a stone bowl. Treat yourself to a Portuguese sundowner wine at INSIDER TIP Wine With a View *(on the left, same opening times as castle). Castle compound: daily, Nov–Feb 9am–6pm, March–Oct 9am–9pm | English-language guided tours 10.30am, 11.30am, 12.30pm, 2pm, 3pm, 4pm, 5pm (in the summer also 6.30pm, 7.30pm) | admission 8.50 euros incl. museum and Câmara Escura (9am–5pm) | castelode saojorge.pt | eléctrico 12, 28 Miradouro de Santa Luzia | bus 737 Chão da Feira*

3 IGREJA DE SANTA ENGRÁCIA/ PANTEÃO NACIONAL ⁄⁄
(135 F4) *(ψ O9)*

The tall white dome of this church, a national pantheon for the great sons and daughters of Portugal who are buried in splendid marble graves, can be seen from afar. It normally takes years for the remains of Portugal's deceased to be moved here. However, the process was speeded up for Portuguese footballing legend Eusebio... an indication that football is the only true religion in Portugal ... Building started in 1570; in 1630, the vestry and paintings inside the church were destroyed. A converted Jew was accused of the crime, and prophesied on the way to the scaffold that the church would never be finished. In fact, the church was eventually dedicated in 1966 – some 400 years after work started. Because of this, the phrase *Obras de Santa Engrácia* (literally Saint Engrácia's works) has become a Portuguese synonym for projects which never see an end.

It is worth exploring the interior to appreciate its harmonious colours and shapes. Steep staris and a lift (only for people with impaired mobility) take visitors up to the terrace around the mighty dome, affording INSIDER TIP amazing views. *Tue–Sun 10am–5pm | admission 4 euros, free on the 1st Sun of the month | Campo de*

Santa Clara | www.igespar.pt | eléctrico 28 Voz Operário

4 IGREJA E MOSTEIRO DE SÃO VICENTE DE FORA ☼
(121 F2) (*∅ 09*)

King Philip II of Spain (Dom Filipe I of Portugal) commissioned the monastery in 1582, and work continued up until the early 18th century. Inside, you'll find marble splendour, choir stalls made from tropical hardwood and blue-and-white azulejos. Today the monastery is the headquarters of the cardinal *(patriarca)* of Lisbon, as well as serving as the burial place for the patriarchs and the kings of the Bragança dynasty. Beautiful views from the terrace. *Tue–Sun 10am–6pm | admission 5 euros | Largo de São Vicente de Fora | eléctrico 28 Voz Operário*

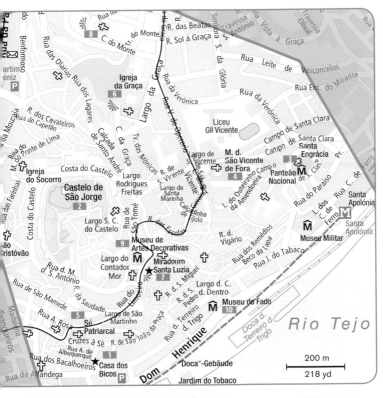

SIGHTSEEING IN ALFAMA, MOURARIA & GRAÇA

1 Casa dos Bicos
2 Castelo de São Jorge
3 Igreja de Santa Engrácia/
   Panteão Nacional
4 Igreja e Mosteiro de São Vicente de Fora
5 Cathedral Sé
6 Miradouro da Graça
7 Miradouro de Santa Luzia/
   Portas do Sol

////// pedestrian zone

8 Miradouro Senhora do Monte
9 Museu de Artes Decorativas
10 Museu do Fado

5 CATHEDRAL SÉ (121 E4) (*📖 N9*)

The cathedral or Sé (short for *sedes episcopalis*, bishopric in English) is the oldest church in Lisbon. Built after the Moors were driven out of the city in 1147, it is said to have replaced a five-naved mosque – to set the new balance of power straight from the start. The cathedral was damaged by various earthquakes, and restored several times over until the beginning of the 20th century. Today, it combines two architectural styles, apparent in the sober Romanesque interior and the elegant Gothic ambulatory with nine chapels. In the garden of the 14th-century Gothic cloisters, archaeological excavations have been going on for years, revealing Roman traces, including the remains of a street and canalisation systems, dating back to the first century. The treasury is reached by the stairs immediately right after the entrance, with relics, robes and a superb golden monstrance from 1760.*Church daily 9am–7pm, cloisters and chapels daily 10am–6pm | admission 2.50 euros | treasury Mon–Fri 10am–1pm, 2–5pm, Sat 10am–5pm | admission 2.50 euros | Mass: Sun 11.30am and 7pm, Tue–Sat 6.30pm | Largo da Sé | eléctrico 28 | bus 37 Sé*

6 MIRADOURO DA GRAÇA (121 E1) (*📖 N8*)

Trees, tables, chairs and a café-kiosk: a favourite meeting place at sunset. Fabulous views across to the castle and the Baixa all the way to the 25 April bridge. *Daily from 10am | eléctrico 28 Largo da Graça*

7 MIRADOURO DE SANTA LUZIA/ PORTAS DO SOL (121 F3) (*📖 N9*)

The viewing terrace *Miradouro de Santa Luzia* offers fine photo opportunities with its bougainvillea and views across the dense sea of rooftops and the maze of alleys that make up Alfama, as well as across the Tagus. The azulejo wall on the *Igreja de Santa Luzia* portrays Lisbon before the earthquake of 1755. A little further up, on the *Largo das Portas do Sol* you'll find a small café kiosk, and just around the corner the chic café ● *Esplanada das Portas do Sol (Sun–Thu 10am–1pm, Fri/Sat 10am–2am). Eléctrico 12, 28 Miradouro de Santa Luzia.*

8 MIRADOURO SENHORA DO MONTE ● (135 E3) (*📖 N8*)

See Lisbon and the Tagus spread out below you from the highest *miradouro* in town. Take a peek into the pilgrimage chapel and ask to be shown the Cadeira de São Gens, the 12th-century stone throne of St Gens, traditionally used by pregnant Portuguese women to pray for an uncomplicated birth. Many visitors take the easy route up the steep hill in a tuk-tuk. The small mobile food carts selling lemonade, coffee and Pasteis de Nata are a new feature. *Eléctrico 28 Rua da Graça*

9 MUSEU DE ARTES DECORATI-VAS ☆ (121 E–F3) (*N9*)

The Espírito Santo family – one of the richest in Portugal – has donated precious items to this museum. Alongside furniture, the museum for applied arts, housed in the noble 17th-century *Palácio Azurara*, shows tapestries and carpets, azulejos, china and silver. Pretty café. *Wed–Mon 10am–5pm | admission 4 euros | Largo das Portas do Sol 2 | www.fress.pt | eléctrico 28 Largo das Portas do Sol*

10 MUSEU DO FADO (135 F5) (*O9*)

An exploration of the history and contemporary role of fado. An audioguide allows visitors to experience the artists and their music, such as virtuoso guitarist Carlos Paredes. The museum's chic restaurant serves modern Portuguese cuisine (*Moderate*). INSIDER TIP In the summer free guided tours in English through the Alfama and the Mouraria. *Tue–Sun 10am–6pm | admission 5 euros | Largo do Chafariz de Dentro 1 | www.museodofado.pt | buses 728, 735, 759, 794 Casa Conto*

BAIXA & AVENIDA

The Baixa – pronounced "baisha" – is downtown Lisbon, rebuilt on the rubble of the devastating earthquake in 1755 from the masterplan of Marquês de Pombal known as the *Baixa Pombalina*. Notable features include wide streets, each one allocated to a different traditional craft, inter-terrace walls built higher than the roof timbers to reduce fire contagion and inside the "Pombaline cage", a symmetrical wood-lattice framework.

The entire architecture is built on stilts on the muddy banks of the Tagus. Baixa is a relatively flat district - so no hills here to tire you out. Many of the splendid Pombaline façades are crumbling over

Great view from a great terrace: Miradouro de Santa Luzia

time, making Baixa an eclectic mixture of freshly renovated buildings next to decaying apartments with weeds growing out of the gutters in the heart of the city. Hidden churches, two or three quirky museums, splendid examples of Lisbon's traditional shopping culture with names of businesses engraved in the cobblestones mix with run-of-the-mill souvenir shops and hotels everywhere you look. The Rua Augusta is the main artery flowing through Baixa where people from around the world converge with restaurant proprietors and street artists. Enjoy an ice-cream at arguably the city's best ice-cream parlour *(Amorino, no. 209, open until midnight in summer)!*

■1 AVENIDA DA LIBERDADE
(120 A–B1) *(Ⓜ L–M 7–8)*

This splendid boulevard forms the bridge between the old and the new Lisboa. At around 1.5 km (1 mile), the Avenida was laid out in 1886 to connect the Praça dos Restauradores with the Praça Marquês

de Pombal. Tree-lined strips of lawn with cafés separate the street from the mosaic-adorned pavements. The boulevard is lined with elegant hotels, boutiques and fancy townhouses, but also has a few eyesores. Pretty: the old wrought-iron kiosks serving a variety of takeaways from seafood to hot dogs. Some, such as the time-out kiosk, even have live music — and the revival of the variety performance park, Parque Mayer, with its brand-new theatre. *Metro (blue) Restauradores, Avenida, Marquês de Pombal*

■2 ELEVADOR DA GLÓRIA
(120 A1–2) *(Ⓜ M9)*

The most central and popular *elevador* has been connecting downtown Baixa with party-central Bairro Alto since 1885, which is why it operates up to midnight. The "valley station" lies on *Praça dos Restauradores* near the tourist information, the "hill station" next to the pretty ☀ viewpoint *Miradouro São Pedro de Alcântara*. *Metro (blue) Restauradores*

SPOTLIGHT ON SPORTS

● A true Lisboeta has to nail their colours to the mast: either red for the Eagles *(Águias)* of Benfica or green for the Lions *(Leões)* of Sporting. For over 100 years, the cult around the two traditional clubs has divided the capital's football fans. Their stadiums, which are less than 3 km (1.5 miles) apart, were both built from scratch for the European Championships in 2004. Benfica's *Estádio da Luz* (Stadium of Light) *(daily except match days 10am–6pm, guided tours every half hour | admission 10 euros | ticket desk Door/Porta 18 | www.sbenfica.pt | metro (blue) Colégio Militar/Luz)* holds about 65,000 spectators, Sporting's

Estádio José Alvalade (daily 9.30am–5pm, on match days until 3/4pm, guided tours 11.30am, 2.30, 3.30, 4.30pm | admission 8 euros, 14 euros incl. museum | www.sporting.pt | metro (yellow) Campo Grande) holds 52,000. On match days, fans from half the country descend on Lisbon hours before kick-off, and the powerful fan clubs get things going. Tickets for league games cost 5–35 euros; order at the stadium ticket desks or online *(daily 10am–8pm | pickup 2 hrs before kick-off at the latest)*. After Bayern Munich, Benfica is the club with the second most registered members worldwide (225,000).

■3 ELEVADOR DO LAVRA
(134 C3) (🞵 M8)

This is the city's oldest *elevador*, dating from 1884. It takes people up to one of the most secluded and least touristy viewpoints in Lisbon, the Jardim de Torel. *Mon–Fri 7.50am–7.55pm, Sat/Sun 9am–7.55pm | metro (blue) Restauradores*

■4 ELEVADOR DE SANTA JUSTA ● ⋇
(120 B3) (🞵 M9)

The undisputed star among Lisbon's *elevadores*, this cast-iron construction is a proper lift. Its spacious wooden cars are pulled up to a height of 30 m (100 ft). It was built by Raul Mesnier de Ponsard, a pupil of Gustave Eiffel's. The elevator was inaugurated in 1902 *(5.15 euros, free with Carris/metro day ticket)*. At the top you'll find a viewing terrace *(admission included in the 5.15 euros, otherwise 1.50 euros)* and the passage onto the Bairro Alto – and the latest project of the great Chiado moderniser Álvaro Siza Vieira: the café terraces below the Carmo church. Here, the Italian restaurant ⋇ *Bella Lisa Elevador (www. bellalisaelevador.com | Moderate)* offers a lunchtime pasta-rodizio buffet. *Daily 7am–11pm, in winter to 9pm | metro (blue, green) Baixa-Chiado*

■5 JARDÍM BOTÂNICO (134 B3) (🞵 L8)

Given a new lease of life in 2017, this green oasis in the middle of the city is the perfect place for relaxing walks. The ancient tropical trees of the garden, which was laid out in 1873, are mainly from the former Portuguese colonies. Ponds, elegant stairways and statues lend the park a charming-picturesque look. *Daily 9am–8pm, butterfly house until 6pm, in winter 9am–6pm | admission 2 euros | Rua da Escola Politécnica 58 | metro (yellow) Rato*

Elevador de Santa Justa: a great shortcut if your feet are tired

■6 MUDE
(120–121 D4) (🞵 M10)

The Museum for Design and Fashion (*mude* meaning both "it is changing" or "change!") is housed in a former bank and presents its permanent exhibition of iconic fashion, furniture and much more in a deliberately post-modern, industrial concrete ambience. The MUDE opened its doors again in autumn 2017: INSIDER TIP now with rooftop terrace. *Tue–Sun 10am–6pm | admission unknown at the time of going to press |*

Take your pick of chairs: design at the MUDE

Rua Augusta 24 | www.mude.pt | metro (blue) Terreiro do Paço

⁊ PARQUE EDUARDO VII ☼
(134 A–B1) (*𝄙 K–L 6–7*)

Long rather than wide, this park extends up the hill behind the Marquês de Pombal square. Fine vistas and photo opportunities from the upper end of the park. On a fine day, the view extends almost to the other bank of the Tagus. Few tourists find their way into the idyllic *Estufas* (hothouses) *(daily, summer 10am–7pm, winter 9am–5pm | admission 3.10 euros, Sun free until 2pm | estufafria.cm-lisboa.pt)* at the top end of the park. *Metro (blue) Marquês de Pombal, Parque*

In close proximity to the Marquês-de-Pombal roundabout, the *Hotel Ritz Four Seasons (open 24 hrs daily | Rua Rodrigo da Fonseca 88 | www.fourseasons.com)* is also popular with art lovers as it's home to a ● INSIDERTIP collection of contemporary Portuguese art exhibiting tapestries, azulejo tiles and paintings (entrance facing away from park). You don't have to consume anything but the *Tea at the Ritz (from 25 euros)* is worth the treat where you can get comfy in one of the chairs and watch the elite guests around you.

⁸ PRAÇA DO COMÉRCIO (TERREIRO DO PAÇO)
(120–121 C–D5) (*𝄙 M–N10*)

When the explorers returned from the new world in the 15th century in their caravels laden with spices, precious metals and slaves, the royal residence relocated from their hillside Castelo to the downtown "Trade Square", also known as *Terreiro do Paço* (Palace Square). The earthquake of 1755 destroyed the enormous palace which originally flanked the west side of the square. The royal family themselves had more luck – they were residing in the far western part of the city when the earthquake hit. At the centre rises the equestrian statue of Joseph I in a heroic pose. But if truth be told, the king spent 20 years in hiding after the earthquake leaving the rebuilding of the destroyed city to his Prime Minister, Marquês de Pombal. The square is flanked by yellow-painted buildings with arcaded walkways which today house restaurants rather than ministry offices. It is an enormous square, ideal for hosting the Pope's mass and other celebrations, from the April 25th memorial concert to the New Year's Eve firework display. The *Patio da Galé* houses the tourist informa-

tion centre and restaurants next to the former city post office in front of which Jewish refugees queued up in the 1940s waiting for their visas, boat tickets and other letters determining their destiny. Opposite, you'll find the *Beer Museum* with (expensive) beers from the former colonies. The *Lisboa Story Centre (daily 10am–8pm | admission 7 euros, family ticket 18 euros | www.lisboastorycentre.*

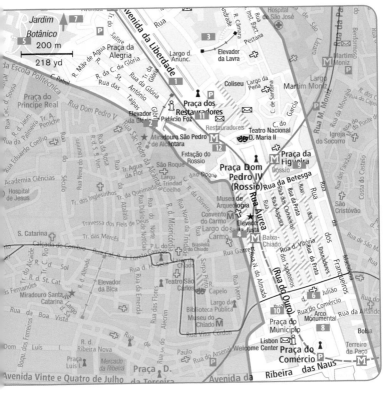

SIGHTSEEING IN BAIXA & AVENIDA

1 Avenida da Liberdade
2 Elevador da Glória
3 Elevador do Lavra
4 Elevador de Santa Justa
5 Jardím Botânico

6 MUDE
7 Parque Eduardo VII
8 Praça do Comércio (Terreiro do Paço)
9 Praça da Figueira

10 Praça do Municipio
11 Praça dos Restauradores
12 Rossio (Praça Dom Pedro IV)

Pedestrian zone

pt | metro (blue) Terreiro do Paço)) takes you on an exciting journey through Lisbon's history.

▣9 PRAÇA DA FIGUEIRA
(120 D4) (𝄞 M9)

Only a row of houses separates this square from Rossio. Its hallmarks are the pigeons fluttering around the equestrian statue of King João I and the young skateboarders. No. 18 houses the city's oldest patisserie, *Confeitaria Nacional*, famous for its delicious *bolo Rei* yeast cake with candied and dried fruit. *Metro (green) Rossio*

▣10 PRAÇA DO MUNICIPIO
(120 C5) (𝄞 M10)

Here stands the city hall *(Paços do Concelho)*, the historical stage for the proclamation of the Republic in 1910, today the seat of the municipality *(Câmara Municipal)*. The neoclassical building is open to visitors every first Sunday of the month at 11am. The twisted double column on the square once served as the local pillory. The money museum, *Museu do Dinheiro,* next door in the secular São Julião church *(www.bportugal.pt)*, shows the history of money. *Eléctrico 15, 18 Praça do Comércio | metro (green, blue) Baixa-Chiado*

▣11 PRAÇA DOS RESTAURADORES
(120 B1) (𝄞 M8–9)

A soaring 30m-high (100 ft) obelisk commemorates the liberation of Portugal from the Spanish yoke in 1640. Today, the day of Victory in the War of Restoration is a national holiday (1 December). Once home to dictator Salazar's propaganda machine, the pink *Palácio Foz* on the edge of the square today welcomes visitors with a tourist information post and the tourist police. Listen out for announcements of **INSIDER TIP** recitals (usually with free admission!) in the first-floor hall of mirrors at 6 or 7pm *(www.gmcs.pt)*. *Metro (blue) Restauradores*

FOR BOOKWORMS & FILM BUFFS

Lisbon Logbook – Witty, charming and with an expert's eye, the late José Cardoso Pires describes the city, its inhabitants and their idiosyncratic ways in short essays

Night Train to Lisbon – Pascal Mercier – the pseudonym of the Swiss philosopher Peter Bieri – published this bestseller in 2004. Bille August's 2012 film adaptation starring Jeremy Irons and Bruno Ganz was heavily criticized in Portugal for its historical inaccurate portrayal of the *resistência* despite its beautiful images and impressive actor performances

Lisbon Story – Filmmaker Wim Wenders, an avowed Lisbon fan, made this film about making a film in Lisbon in 1994. Atmospheric backdrops and the music by Portuguese band Madredeus make this movie well worth seeing

São Jorge (Saint George) – Portugal in hard financial times. A boxer is forced to work as a debt collector. Sensitively narrated film (2016) – the camera captures the decaying beauty of derelict high-rises and barracks on the south banks of the Tagus. The main character won Best Actor in Venice.

12 ROSSIO ★ (120 B–C2) *(𝄞 M9)*

Hear the heartbeat of the city in this popular square, which is always thronged with people and full of life. The square, which is paved in an ● artistic wave mosaic, is flanked by the long-established cafés *Suiça* (often beleaguered by buskers) and *Nicola*. The northern side is occupied by the neoclassical national theatre *Dona Maria II (a peek behind the scenes, also in English: Mon 11am, except in Aug, www.teatro-dmaria.pt)*. To the right, set a little bit back from the square, stands the *Igreja São Domingos,* where the Inquisition once sat in judgement. Stone monuments in front of the church commemorate the 1506 pogrom against the Jews, which started here. Between Rossio and Restauradores you'll find the neo-Manueline Rossio Train Station, with its pretty horse-shoe shaped entrances and a *Starbucks*. Around Rossio, several tiny bars vie to serve the *Ginginja* cherry liqueur, whose popularity transcends generations and social class. *Metro (green) Rossio*

Victory column: obelisk on the Praça dos Restauradores

CHIADO & BAIRRO ALTO

While Chiado proper covers just a few streets, much of the city's artistic soul resides here.

For centuries, the "Meridian of the literati", as the Lisbon author José Cardoso Pires (1925–1998) called it, was the meeting point for artists, fashion designers, dandys, poets and intellectuals. Here you'll find a bronze figure of Portugal's most famous writer Fernando Pessoa sitting in front of one of his favourite cafés, *A Brasileira*, as well as the *São Carlos* opera, several splendid theatres and the best antiquarian bookshops in town. When, in August 1988, a major fire destroyed a large chunk of Chiado, the whole of Lisbon was under shock for days. The adjacent *Bairro Alto* quarter is Lisbon's traditional party zone. Alongside pubs, restaurants, bars and clubs, one-off shops with long opening hours ensure a steady flow of visitors. In the daytime, the Old Town quarter shows a different face of pleasant peace and calm.

1 IGREJA DO CARMO (120 B3) *(𝄞 M9)*

Visible from afar, the ruined Carmo church rises high above the Old Town as a stone memento mori. The great Gothic 14th-century convent was all but de-

Peace at last among the ruins of Igreja do Carmo

stroyed by the 1755 earthquake. All that remained standing were the elegant columns of the entrance arch. The roofless church houses the archaeological museum. The church lies on leafy Largo do Carmo with a small playful fountain and a café. New: there's now also **INSIDER TIP** a café on the Carmo terraces. *Mon–Sat 10am–6pm, Oct–April only until 5pm | admission 4 euros | Largo do Carmo 4 | www.museuarqueologicodocarmo.pt | metro (blue, green) Baixa-Chiado*

▣ IGREJA SÃO ROQUE ★
(120 A2) (*Ⳛ M9*)

Built in 1566 on the site of a Plague cemetery, the Jesuit church survived the 1755 earthquake nearly undamaged. The most splendid of the eight lateral chapels is the one dedicated to John the Baptist *(Capela de São João Baptista)* on the left, near the altar. King João V commissioned it in 1742 from Rome. The best artists were commissioned and only the most precious materials used – Carrara marble, ivory, gold,

blue lapislazuli, purple amethysts... After being blessed by the Pope, the chapel was shipped to Lisbon in individual parts to be rebuilt in situ during several years of work. The adjacent *Museu de São Roque (April–Sept Mon 2–7pm, Tue–Sun 10am–7pm, Thu until 8pm, Oct–March until 6pm | admission 2.50 euros, Sun until 2pm free | Thu 3pm, Fri 11.30am and 4.30pm, Sat 10am, Sun 3pm free guided tour with ticket | www.museudesaoroque. com)* boasts the second-largest collection of relics on the Iberian peninsula. *Church: April–Sept Mon 2–7pm, Tue–Sun 9am–7pm, Thu until 8pm, Oct–March until 6pm| admission free | Largo Trindade Coelho | metro (blue) Baixa-Chiado, Restauradores, then Elevador da Glória | eléctrico 28 Largo do Camões*

▣ **INSIDER TIP** ▶ MIRADOURO DE SANTA CATARINA ☼
(134 B5) (*Ⳛ L10*)

This viewing terrace, with its far-reaching views across the port and the Tagus, was made for balmy summer nights. Below the café kiosk next to the Adamastor sculpture *(daily from noon, depending on the weather),* is a meeting point for a youthful alternative scene. Also great: the beautiful terrace of the child-friendly *Noobai* café next door. *Eléctrico 28 Calhariz-Bica | metro (blue, green) Baixa-Chiado*

■4 MIRADOURO SÃO PEDRO DE ALCÂNTARA ● ⚭
(120 A1–2) (*ω L–M9*)

Wooden benches under shady trees, a gently bubbling fountain, and an open-air café – this is a good place to take a break before continuing to the trendy Príncipe Real quarter. Fabulous views take in Old Lisbon with Mouraria and Alfama, the church towers and domes and the Castelo de São Jorge. *Metro (blue) Restauradores, then Elevador da Glória*

■5 MUSEU NACIONAL DE ARTE CONTEMPORÂNEA DO CHIADO
(120 B5) (*ω M1*)

Lisbon's museum for contemporary art is housed in the restored *Convento de S. Francisco.* A permanent collection of Portuguese art from the mid-19th century onwards is supplemented by excellent changing exhibitions of modern art and photography. There is also a pretty self-service café in the sculpture garden. *Tue–Sun 10am–6pm | admission 4.50 euros, free on the 1st Sun of the month | Rua Serpa Pinto 4 | www.museuartecontemporanea.pt | metro (blue, green) Baixa-Chiado*

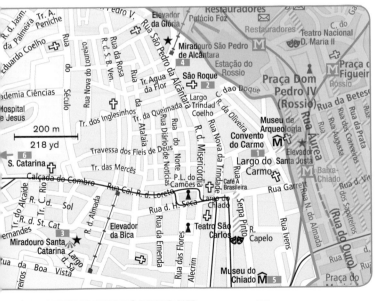

SIGHTSEEING IN CHIADO & BAIRRO ALTO

- **1** Igreja do Carmo
- **2** Igreja São Roque
- **3** Miradouro de Santa Catarina
- **4** Miradouro São Pedro de Alcântara
- **5** Museu Nacional de Arte Contemporânea do Chiado
- **6** Museu Júlio Pomar

▨ Pedestrian zone

6 MUSEU JÚLIO POMAR
(134 B4) (𝌆 L9)

The studio-museum of Júlio Pomar (born in 1926), one of Portugal's best contemporary artists, exhibits 100 works from his various creative periods (Neo Realism, Neo Expressionism). The light rooms were redesigned by the acclaimed architect Siza Vieira. INSIDER TIP If you come on Tue, you'll get in free! *Tue–Sun 10am–6pm | admission 2 euros | Rua do Vale 7 | www.ateliermuseujuliopomar.pt | metro (blue, green) Baixa-Chiado*

CAMPO DE OURIQUE, LAPA & MADRAGOA

The quiet neighbourhood of Campo de Ourique emerged in the late 19th century. Pretty Art Nouveau façades, welcoming cafés and pretty shops are what make this mainly residential quarter so charming.

Lapa, near the Basílica da Estrela, is Lisbon's most well-heeled neighbourhood and the main embassy quarter. The adjoining small district of *Madragoa* – with its secluded alleyways, little old churches and idyllic small squares – is one of Lisbon's nicest Old Town quarters. The eléctrico 25 trundles through some beautiful streets.

■ ASSEMBLEIA DA REPÚBLICA
(133 F2–3) (𝌆 K9)

At the *Palácio de São Bento,* the Portuguese parliament sits when it is in session. The Prime Minister's offices are to the rear. Wide free-standing staircases, flanked by marble lions, lead up to the palace (19th century), built on the ruins of the Benedictine monastery of São Bento de Saúde. Impressive set of neoclassical columns at the main entrance. *Av. Dom Carlos | www.parlamento.pt | eléctrico 28 Calçada Estrela*

In search of the "real" Lisbon: in the old city district of Madragoa

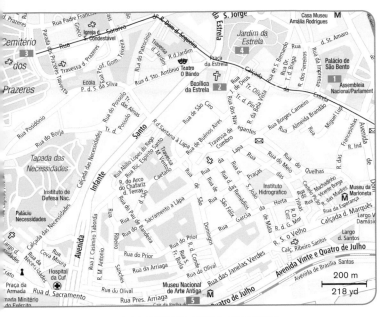

SIGHTSEEING IN CAMPO DE OURIQUE, LAPA & MADRAGOA

▨▨▨ Pedestrian zone

1 Assembleia da República
3 Cemitério dos Prazeres
5 Museu Nacional de Arte Antiga
2 Basílica da Estrela
4 Jardim da Estrela

▨ BASÍLICA DA ESTRELA ☼
(133 E2) (*∭ J9*)

The white dome of the "Basilica of the Star" stands out on Lisbon's skyline. Go up there for great panoramic views *(admission to the dome 4 euros)*. Queen Maria I (1734–1816) donated the basilica in 1777 in gratitude for the birth of a male heir to the throne. Today, it is much in demand for the funerals of the rich and famous. Particularly beautiful is the neo-classical main façade with marble statues *(Mon 7.30am–1pm, 4–7.45pm, Tue/Thu 7.30am–7.45pm, Wed 7.30am–1pm, 3–7.45pm, Fri 7.30am–1pm, 3–7.45pm, Sat 9.30am–7.45pm, Sun 8.30am–1pm, 3–7.45pm)*. The enormous nativity scene sculpted by baroque master Machado de Castro *(admission 2 euros)* is also well worth the visit – over 400 figurines depict the stable in Bethlehem, surrounded by a traditional Portuguese scenery, combining realistic and rustic elements. *Eléctrico 25, 28 Estrela*

▨ CEMITÉRIO DOS PRAZERES
(132 C2–3) (*∭ H9*)

The huge *Cemetery of the Pleasures*, laid out in 1833, is a small city in itself. In death, magnificent mausoleums and modest graves rub shoulders. Many famous Portuguese found their last place of rest here, but most visitors come to see the plots dedicated to different vocations and the vast diversity of grave designs. Senhor Licinio Fidalgo, a very friendly historian, is available to answer questions; ask for him at the entrance. *Oct–April dai-*

ly 9am–5pm, May–Sept 9am–6pm | Praça São João Bosco | Parada dos Prazeres | terminus eléctrico 28 25 Rua Saraiva de Carvalho | bus 709 Rua Saraiva de Carvalho

4 JARDIM DA ESTRELA
(133 E2) (*ΜΜ J–K9*)

Small urban park in front of the *Basílica da Estrela* with ancient trees, wooden benches under plane trees, a small terrace café and ponds. At its centre stands a filigree Art Nouveau music pavilion. It's not far from the garden's top exit to the Rua de São Bento flanked with delightful stores and home to the last residence of the fado queen, Amália Rodrigues *(no. 193, www.amaliarodrigues.pt)*. *Praça da Estrela | eléctrico 25, 28 Estrela*

5 MUSEU NACIONAL DE ARTE
ANTIGA ☆ (133 E4) (*ΜΜ J10*)

The National Museum of Ancient Art has Portugal's most important art collection. Housed stylishly in the palace of an Indian Viceroy from the 17th century, its objects tell stories, be it Japanese folding screens with depictions of Portuguese as "longnoses" on ships, or furniture, ceramics, glass, sacred art, silver and gold work, as well as Oriental objects in ivory and mother-of-pearl. It also has an exceptional collection of European masters, with works by Dürer, Holbein, Cranach and Velasquez. The most important pieces are the six-piece winged altar by the Portuguese Early Renaissance painter Nuno Gonçalves and Hieronymus Bosch's powerful triptych *The Temptation of Saint Anthony* — not recommended if you suffer from nightmares! But there's a beautiful ☆ terrace bar for views across the river and the port. *Tue 2–6pm, Wed–Sun 10am–6pm | admission 6 euros, free on the 1st Sun of the month | Rua das Janelas Verdes 95 | www.museudearteantiga.pt | eléctrico 15 Cais Rocha | bus 714 Cais Rocha*

Next door, in the *Jardim 9 de Abril*, you'll find the ☆ bistro/café cocktail bar *Le Chat (Mon–Sat 12.30–2pm, Sun 12.30pm–midnight | www.lechat-lisboa. com)*, a trendy spot for a sundowner with superb views across the river.

LOW BUDGET

Free admissions to museums on Sundays enjoyed a welcome comeback in 2017: Culture for free until 2pm in the city's national museums and monuments.

Fancy a family-friendly football afternoon with a view of the Tagus? Head for the Restelo stadium of the second-league team "Belenenses": *Estádio de Restelo* **(130 B–C4)** (*ΜΜ C10–11*) *(Av. do Restelo | Belém | www.osbelenenses.pt | tickets on site 7–15 euros)*

BELÉM, RESTELO & AJUDA

In Belém (Bethlehem), approx. 7 km/4 miles west of the city centre, you can discover some of the top sights of the capital, including the Hieronymus Monastery (Mosteiro dos Jerónimos) or the Torre de Belém.

The earthquake of 1755 spared this part of town. Thus, after the disaster, Belém and the adjacent quarters of Restelo and Ajuda became a sought-after residential quarter for the nobility and other wealthy citizens. This hasn't changed much since.

Visible from afar even today: the Hieronymus Monastery

At the heart of Belém, the pink *Palácio de Belém* has been the seat of the Portuguese president since the founding of the Republic in 1910. Until the proclamation of the Republic, the royal family lived not far from here, at the *Palácio Nacional da Ajuda*. The palace, which was never quite completed, is well worth visiting; it adjoins the *Jardim Botânico da Ajuda (www.jardimbotanicodaajuda.com)*, Portugal's oldest botanical gardens.

■ MAAT ★ (131 E5) (*∅ E12*)

Lisbon's answer to the Tate Modern: With its impressive arched structure, the museum for architecture, art and technology is the new riverfront star on the banks of the Tagus. This imposing building with its exciting series of installations and dialogues between architects and artists is a great destination to explore after a 7 km/4.3 miles long walk along the river from the *Torre de Belém* (see p. 49) or *Mosteiro dos Jerónimos* (see p. 45) to the Cais do Sodré. The former

electricity museum in the red-brick building is now also a part of the MAAT. *Wed–Mon noon–8pm | admission MAAT 5 euros, electricity museum (Central) 5 euros, joint ticket 9 euros | Av. Brasília/Central Tejo | tel. 2 10 02 81 30 | www.maat.pt | eléctrico 15 Belém | buses 714, 727, 728, 729, 751 Belém*

■ MOSTEIRO DOS JERÓNIMOS ★ (130 B–C5) (*∅ C11*)

It was intended that the Hieronymus Monastery would be the first thing those coming to Lisbon by ship would see. The glory of the Golden Age of the Portuguese Discoveries, and the last place of rest for the great and good of the country, since 1983 the monastery has also been a Unesco World Heritage site. King Manuel I, named the Fortunate *(o Venturoso)*, as his mariners brought him back an empire, laid the first stone for the monastery in 1501. Inspired by the stories told by the seafarers, his architects created extravagant oriental deco-

Golden, but also exhausting times: royal rowboat from 1780 at the Museu da Marinha

rations. Only centuries later would this idiosyncratic architectural style, between Gothic and Renaissance, be given the name '"Manueline". After King Manuel's death in 1521, it took almost another 50 years for the monastery to be finished.

The first features to hit the eye are the two ornate portals, masterpieces of stonemasonry. Inside the church, six slender and richly decorated pillars turn into palm trees, with a sky of stars and squares. Bellow the gallery you'll see two splendid sarcophagi. The one containing the mortal remains of Vasco da Gama is decorated with caravels, a globe and the Crusader cross; the other, to the right, of national bard Luís de Camões, is decorated with a quill, laurel wreath and lyre. The author of the Portuguese national epic *Os Lusíadas* doesn't actually lie here, however; he died of the plague in 1580, completely destitute, and was buried in a Lisbon mass grave.

The royal sarcophagi stand inside deep niches at the magnificent high altar, carried by marble elephants. The two-level

● cloisters are an architectural fairytale. With their rampant filigree ornamentation, they are considered among the most beautiful in the world – a fitting environment for the tomb of Fernando Pessoa, the great Modernist poet. The refectory next to the cloisters has extremely fine fan vaulting and pretty azulejo panels from the 18th century telling the story of Joseph and his brothers – a tragic and exciting comic. INSIDERTIP Tue–Fri at noon you can catch English-language tours at no extra cost! *Cloisters: Oct–April Tue–Sun 10am–5.30pm, May–Sept Tue–Sun 10am–6.30pm | admission 10 euros, free Sun, church: admission free | Praça do Império | www.mosteirojeronimos.pt | eléctrico 15 | train from Cais do Sodré to Belém*

3 MUSEU DA MARINHA ★
(130 B5) (*ℳ C11–12*)

The Maritime Museum is filled with model ships from ancient to contemporary: fishing boats, whalers, rowing galleys, frigates, caravels, sailing yachts, cruise liners, warships, oil tankers. The museum is a 150 years old monument to Portugal's seafaring history and the Age of Discoveries. Also on display are maps, nautical instruments, log books and paintings. Only a few hundred metres away is the spot where Captain Vasco da Gama put to sea, over 500 years ago. *Summer Tue–Sun 10am–6pm, winter Tue–Sun 10am–5pm | admission 6.50 euros, free on the 1st Sun of the month | Praça do Império | museu.marinha.pt | eléctrico 15 CCB*

4 MUSEU NACIONAL DE ARQUEOLOGIA (130 B–C5) (*ᗝ C11*)

One of the most interesting sections of the Archaeological Museum, which is wrongly disregarded, is the treasury.

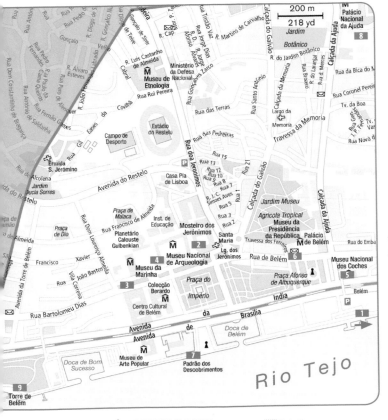

Jewellery and coins from between 20 and 150 AD attest to the rich gold, silver and copper deposits Portugal once had. The mines were exploited to near-exhaustion under the Romans. There are also ancient archaeological finds, artefacts from Egypt, Roman mosaics and medieval tools. The museum is housed in the western wing of the *Hieronymus Monastery*. *Tue–Sun 10am–6pm | admission 5 euros, free on the 1st Sun of the month | Praça do Império | www.museuarqueologia.pt | eléctrico 15 Mosteiro dos Jerónimos*

5 MUSEU NACIONAL DOS COCHES
● (131 D5) (*🕮 D11*)

The upper-class have always preferred a sophisticated means of transport and the striking, "elevated" coach museum dazzles visitors with its collection of 16th to 20th century noble carriages, travel coaches and royal vehicles in an ultra-modern space.The Lisbon Riding School has returned to its original residence in the former museum building opposite. *Tue–Sun 10am–6pm | admission 6 euros | Praça Afonso de Albuquerque | www.museudoscoches.pt | eléctrico 15 Belém | buses 714, 727 Belém, among others*

6 MUSEU DA PRESIDÊNCIA
(131 D5) (*🕮 D11*)

At the powdery pink Belém Palace you'll meet Portugal's presidents in the gallery, from the first one, the modest intellectual Manuel Arriaga, who hated to see money wasted (1910), to Marcelo Rebelo da Sousa, in office since 2016. Come **INSIDER TIP** on a Saturday, when you can take in the palace, the gardens and the Virgin Mary Cycle of the artist, Paula Rego. As with visits to all official buildings, it is recommended to phone beforehand! *Museum Tue–Sun 10am–6pm | admission 2.50 euros (free Sun until 1pm); palace and gardens Sat 10.30am–5.30pm | 5 euros | Praça Afonso de Albuquerque| tel. 213 61 46 60 | www.museu.presidencia.pt | eléctrico 15 Belém*

7 PADRÃO DOS DESCOBRIMENTOS
☀ (130 C6) (*🕮 C12*)

Symbolising the departure of the Portuguese explorers for new worlds, this huge white monument was erected in Belém in 1960 to commemorate Prince Henry the Seafarer (*Infante Dom Henrique*, 1394–1460), on the occasion of the 500-year anniversary of his death. At 50 m (164 ft) high, the monument pushes out into the Tagus like the prow of a caravel. On top of it stands Henry. Clustering behind him are important personalities of the day: captains, cartographers, astronomers, painters, monks, writers. A lift takes visitors up to the viewing platform, for the best view over the large marble mosaic on the ground in front of the monument. It shows a map of the world with the former Portuguese colonies. *March Tue–Sun 10am–7pm, April–Sept daily 10am–7pm, Oct–Feb Tue–Sun 10am–6pm | admission 4 euros | www.padraodosdescobrimentos.pt | eléctrico 15 Centro Cultural Belém*

8 PALÁCIO NACIONAL DA AJUDA
(131 D2–3) (*🕮 D10*)

A hidden gem for moments when you want to flee the madding crowds. To escape the city after the 1755 earthquake, King José I had a temporary building erected here. While King João VI commissioned the palace in 1802, it was 1862 by the time King Luís I moved into the new royal residence with his queen Dona Maria Pia. It was never truly finished. The young, artistic queen took responsibility for designing the interior, and the palace is exquisitely furnished with

Marble mosaic in front of Padrão dos Descobrimentos mapping Portugal's former colonies

unusual antiquities and works of art. In the pink-hued Saxon Hall, even the chairs and tables are manufactured from Meissen porcelain. *Thu–Tue 10am–5.30pm | admission 5 euros, free on the 1st Sun of the month | www.palaciodaajuda.pt | eléctrico 18 Calçada Ajuda (Palácio)*

▩ 9 TORRE DE BELÉM ★ ⋇
(130 A6) (*U B12*)

This defensive tower in fine Manueline style is a reminder of the time when the Portuguese explorers started their sea journeys on caravels from here. Built under the aegis of King Manuel I between 1515 and 1521, the tower served as a welcoming symbol for ships coming back from all corners of the world, laden with goods, and for defending the wide mouth of the river. The original position of this historic gem with its stone rope, folding domes and Venetian loggias used to be on a small island in the middle of the Tagus. Over the course of the centuries, the river silted up, so that today the Torre is accessible from the shore. A short footbridge leads inside, past a few cannons, and on to the terrace with the statue of the patron saint of success, Madona do Bom Sucesso, who used to greet the ships of the explorers. From a height of 35 m (115 ft) a terrace on the fourth floor affords a good view of the surroundings and the river. In high season it gets fairly claustrophobic up here. *Oct–April Tue–Sun 10am–5.30pm, May–Sept Tue–Sun 10am–6.30pm | admission 3 euros, free on the 1st Sun of the month | www.torrebelem.pt | eléctrico 15 Largo da Princesa*

OUTSIDE THE CITY CENTRE

AQUEDUTO DAS ÁGUAS LIVRES
(129 D2–3) (*U H6*)

The *Aqueduct of the Free Waters* is one of the most imposing icons of the capital. Even though Lisbon is practically surrounded by the delta of the river Tagus, lack of drinking water was the city's main problem for centuries. While King D. João V. (1705–1750) commissioned the aqueduct, his people paid for it with a water tax. The water was channelled across 18 km (11 miles) both below and above ground to the *MãedʼÁgua* (Mother of the Water) reservoir close to today's Amoreiras shopping centre. Miraculously, the monumental structure survived the earthquake of 1755 intact, and the aqueduct remained in use until 1967. Spanning just under 1 km (half a mile), the section that bridges the Alcântara Valley forms the most impressive part of the structure. It consists of 35 arches, the tallest of which is 65 m (213 ft) high and 29 m (95 ft) wide. The footpath across the aqueduct is once again open to pedestrians. While it can only be crossed in one direction, it offers excellent views. *1 March–30 Nov Tue–Sat 10am–6pm | admission 2.50 euros | Calçada da Quintinha 6 | www.epal.pt | bus 702 from Marquês de Pombal to Cç. Mestres*

A familiar figure? Cristo Rei is a replica of the statue of Christ in Rio

CRISTO REI (138 C4) (*O*)
With his gaze fixed firmly towards Lisbon, the statue of Christ on the southern banks of the Tagus receives his visitors with open arms. For some, the *Christ King* is a place of pilgrimage, but most people come here for the spectacular views over Lisbon and the delta of the Tagus. A lift whisks visitors up 80 m (262 ft) to the viewing platform supporting the 28 m-high (92 ft) concrete statue. Inaugurated in 1959, the figure of Christ, a copy of the Redemptor in Rio de Janeiro, was erected in gratitude for Portugal having been spared the World War II. *In winter daily 9.30am–6.15pm, in summer Mon–Fri 9.30am–6.30pm, Sat/Sun until 7pm | admission 4 euros, July–mid Oct 5 euros | www.cristorei.pt | ferry from Cais do Sodré to Cacilhas, then bus 101 to Cristo Rei*

MUSEU CALOUSTE GULBENKIAN ★ (124 A4) (*K5*)
The city's largest museum is also the most beautiful. The Gulbenkian shows part of

the unique art collection that Armenian oil magnate Calouste Sarkis Gulbenkian bequeathed to Lisbon, which had provided him with a safe haven during World War II. Half of the exhibition shows Oriental applied arts and crafts – tapestries, azulejos, carpets, books and manuscripts, porcelain and glassware from Turkey, Persia, Syria and China. Further rooms display paintings and sculptures of European masters. You'll find works by Rubens, Rembrandt, Frans Hals, Turner, Gainsborough, Manet, Degas, Renoir and Rodin, as well as period furniture, porcelain and silver tableware, most of them masterpieces in the 18th-century French tradition. Fans of Art Nouveau may want to spend a large part of their visit in the room dedicated to René Lalique. The *cafetaria* with outdoor dining has recently been refurbished and the quality of the food is first-rate. For an extra 7 euros, you can take INSIDER TIP an English-language tour through the universe of "Mr Five Percent" every Monday at 10:30am. The tour provides a real insight in art history. Afterwards give yourself time to wander through the rooms.

A stroll among locals through the pretty ● Gulbenkian gardens and a visit to the adjacent *Centro de Arte Moderna* (Museum of Modern Art, *www.cam.gulbenkian.pt),* which provides an overview of the modern and contemporary art scene in Portugal, are well worth it. *Wed–Mon 10am–6pm | admission 5 euros, free admission on Sun, combination ticket with Centro de Arte Moderna and all temporary exhibitions 15 euros | Av. de Berna 45a | www.museu.gulbenkian.pt | metro (blue) São Sebastião, Praça de Espanha*

MUSEU DE LISBOA – PALÁCIO PIMENTA (138 C3) *(𝄞 O)*
This is the story of the city from antiquity to the current day – from Roman ampho-

rae for fish sauce to an interactive 3D model showing Lisbon before the 1755 earthquake. The museum is housed in the *Palácio Pimenta*, which King João V had erected in 1746 as a present for his mistress. The inside of the palace alone, with its furniture and splendid azulejos, as well as the beautiful old palace kitchen, is well worth visiting. Exceptional: the free *Jardim Bordallo* (see p. 102) with fabulously surreal animal sculptures. *Tue–Sun 10am–6pm | admission 3 euros, Sun until 1pm free | Campo Grande 245 | www.museudelisboa.pt | metro (yellow, green) Campo Grande*

MUSEU NACIONAL DO AZULEJO ★
(137 D3–4) *(𝄞 P–Q7)*
This tile museum really is a must-see. Download the free app at the entrance; it replaces the audio guide and tells you all about the extensive collection of the art of tile painting that is so typical of Portugal – from Moorish beginnings into the 21st century. An azulejo panorama 35 m (115 ft) long and showing Lisbon before the earthquake occupies pride of place in the collection.

The museum is housed in the *Convento da Madre de Deus.* The Poor Clares convent was built in 1509 by Leonor, the "perfect princess" – one of the richest women of her time but also a very modest lady: When you enter this sublime church decorated in paintings, exquisite azulejos and gold-smothered woodcarvings, you walk over her grave. Visitors are also attracted by the café-restaurant's special charm. On hot days, this is a lovely, restful spot shaded by palm trees. Book in advance *(servicosedu cativo@mnazulejo.dgpc.pt or by phone)* to take part in a INSIDER TIP one-hour workshop to paint your own tile *(Mon–Fri 12 euros, Sat, Sun 15 euros, 10am–5pm)* ready for you to collect 2–3 days later. *Tue–Sun 10am–6pm | admission 5 euros, free on the 1st Sun of the month | Rua Madre de Deus 4 | tel. 2 18 10 03 40 | www.museudoazulejo.pt | buses 759, 794 Igreja Madre Deus*

MUSEU DO ORIENTE (132 C5) *(ⴰ H11)*

The imposing Museum of the Orient housed in a former codfish warehouse tells the story of the Portuguese presence in Asia. Antiquities, paintings and art objects illustrate the great era of the Portuguese explorers. On display are costumes, puppets, masks, paintings and ritual items. The museum also puts on a varied cultural programme of workshops, music, theatre, dance, cinema and changing exhibitions, plus an Oriental restaurant. *Tue–Sun 10am–6pm, Fri 10am–10pm (guided tour Sun 4pm) | admission 6 euros, Fri 6–10pm free | Av. de Brasília | Doca de Alcântara | www.museudooriente.pt | eléctrico 15, 18, Alcântara Mar (Museu Oriente)*

PALÁCIO DOS MARQUESES DE FRONTEIRA (128 B1) *(ⴰ G5)*

The romantic gardens are what most draw the eye in this noble palace in the Benfica part of town. The first Marquis of Fronteira commissioned the palace in the 17th century, initially as a hunting pavilion. Particularly impressive are the azulejos. Deities, planets, signs of the zodiac, birds, cats and monkeys adorn benches and façades on the veranda. The magnificently tiled Kings Gallery dominates the lower part of the gardens. The azujelos shine deep dark blue in the sun and find their reflection in the pond in front. *Only accessible on a guided tour, June–Sept Mon–Sat 10.30, 11, 11.30am, noon, Oct–May Mon–Sat 11am and noon | admission palace and gardens 7.50, gardens 3 euros | Largo São Domingos de Benfica 1 | www.fronteira-alorna.pt | metro (blue) Jardim Zoológico | then bus 770 Palácio Fronteira | or by taxi*

PARQUE DAS NAÇÕES ★ (123 E–F 1–4) *(ⴰ S1–4)*

The former Expo area has become a symbol for the new Lisbon. The World Exposition of 1998 formed part of a gigantic urbanisation project. A new neighbourhood emerged on the banks of the Tagus, practically from wasteland; today, some 20,000 people live and work here. This is also where you'll find Lisbon's gems of contemporary architecture, like pearls on a string. The 17 km (10 miles) *Ponte Vasco da Gama* spans the wide Tagus delta. An architectural highlight is the high-tech train station of *Oriente*: a filigree palm grove made from steel and glass, designed by Spanish star architect Santiago Calatrava. The number one attraction in the Park of Nations is the gigantic *Oceánário* (see p. 103), one of the largest marine aquariums in Europe. The shimmering and energy-efficient mosaic covering on the south wing is reminiscent of fish scales.

The futuristic *Pavilhão Atlântico (MEO Arena)* can hold 20,000 people for concerts and sports events. Next door you'll find the trade fair grounds of *FIL Feira Internacional de Lisboa*. Alongside numerous bars and pubs, the *Casino Lisboa,* which also stages (free) shows and has a luxury restaurant, draws visitors in the evening. To explore the area more actively, hire bikes or kayaks (for the Oceánário basin) *(www.marinaparquedasnacoes. pt)*. A new attraction parked at the exit of the Vasco-da-Gama Shopping Centre is the Sitgos *(15 euros/hr. | www.sitgo.pt)*, a type of electric scooter. *www.portaldas nacoes.pt | metro (red) Oriente*

PARQUE FLORESTAL DE MONSANTO (128 A–C 1–6) *(ⴰ C–G 5–10)*

This huge park in the northwest of Lisbon is the city's green lung. It boasts endless biking, hiking and riding trails, picnic spots, playgrounds, fitness trails and a few restaurants. There are also free-climbing and skating facilities. Monsanto also forms part of the 14 km (8.5 miles) long ● *Biodiversity Route (Rota da Biodiversidade | www.cm-lisboa.pt/viver/ambiente/parque-florestal-de-monsanto/rota-da-biodiversidade),* leading past places of interest for history, natural history and ecology – chapels, palaces, geo monuments. The starting point is in Belém. *Bus 729 from Belém to Montes Claros*

the rail track for the train connection with the south of Portugal underneath the road was added in 1999.

BEACHES

Some lisboetas prefer the beaches to the west (138 A–B4) *(⺫ 0),* others swear by the miles of dune-fringed ● *Costa da Caparica* (138 C4–5) *(⺫ 0),* extending south from the resort of Caparica on the southern banks of the Ta-

Gazing at the beauties: the tile museum in the Madre de Deus monastery

PONTE 25 DE ABRIL
(132 B6) *(⺫ G11–12)*

The elegant Ponte 25 *(Vinte e cinco)* de Abril is strongly reminiscent of the Golden Gate Bridge in San Francisco. Dictator Salazar bestowed his own name on the bridge when it was inaugurated in 1966. After the regime was toppled, the bridge was given its current name to commemorate the Carnation Revolution of 25 April 1974. The five-lane highway across the river is at a height of 70 m (230 ft);

gus. In summer, a Noddy train runs between the town and the fishing village of Fonte da Telha. Every stop in between has a beach bar; the *Waikiki (stop no. 15 | Praia da Sereia)* is a meeting place for surfers and windsurfers, chic *Borda de Água (no. 14)* is a favourite with the Lisbon jetset, no. 16 has a kitesurf school with rental *(www.katavento.net, www.bordadagua.com.pt).* The stretch of beach at no. 19 is a meeting point for gays and nudists.

Take a break from city life and head for the coast to the Cabo da Roca

DAY TRIPS

ESTORIL/CASCAIS (138 A3–4) (*illustration O*)

On the coast 25 km (15 miles) west of Lisbon, Estoril and Cascais used to be the seaside resorts of choice for kings and nobility. The train ride from Lisbon's Cais do Sodré station takes only half an hour or so, but it's worth allocating a whole day to visit the resorts, if you don't want to rush it. Bring swimming togs!

Estoril is famous, and not only for having the biggest casino in Europe. During World War II, the town was swarming with spies, as well as receiving many prominent personalities and royalty. From Estoril, you can take a wonderful walk along the beach promenade to Cascais.

Cascais has managed to hold on to the charm of its historic centre. The vibrant old part of Cascais – which, by the way, is home to a sizeable British and Irish population – has many bars, restaurants and boutiques. The City Hall (*Câmara Municipal*) boasts a fine *azulejo* façade and a nice and free exhibition (also in English) about the town's history. On the southern shore, the mighty citadel juts out into the sea. Here and at the station, you can rent bikes for free (*www.cm-cascais.pt*).

The municipal park leads on to the maritime museum, *Museu do Mar (Tue–Sun 10am–5pm / admission free),* which tells the story of the region's fishing traditions. Next door, in the chimney building, the *Paula Rego Museum (Tue–Sun 10am–5/6pm / admission 3 euros / www.casa dashistoriaspaularego.com)* celebrates the fascinating work of the London-based Portuguese artist.

A 1 km (half a mile) walk along the coast road leads to the natural spectacle of *Boca do Inferno,* the 20 m (65 ft) deep "jaws of hell". 5 km (3 miles) north, discover one of Portugal's most beautiful beaches – the *Praia do Guincho,* known to windsurfers the world over. One of their favourite meeting spots is the *Bar do Guincho (daily to late at night)* right on the beach. Information: *www.visitcascais.com*

SINTRA (138 B3) (*∅ O*)

This picturesque little town lies at the foot of the Sintra hills, 20 km (12 miles) west of Lisbon. Royal palaces and stately homes, parks and gardens – only a 45-minute train ride from Lisbon's Rossio station. Admission prices are steep though. Enquire about cheaper multi-entry tickets *(www.parquesdesintra.pt)*. One minute away from the station on the left-hand side is the *Café Saudade (www. saudade.pt)* with guesthouse – it's worth spending one night in this small town. Great for monarchy nostalgians: the new INSIDER TIP *Palácio de Sintra – Bed & Breakfast (Rua Consiglieri Pedroso 23 | tel. 21 34 20 51 | www.portugal-collection.com | Budget)*

Sintra's emblem, the *Palácio Nacional de Sintra (Thu–Tue 9.30am–6/7pm | admission 10 euros)* stands out with its huge conical chimneys. For generations, this 16th-century palace was used as a summer residence by Portugal's royal family. A reminder of that era are the unique tiled walls *(azulejos)* telling so many stories that a guided tour *(daily 2.30pm, 5 euros)* is highly recommended. High above Sintra, there's not only the ruins of the Moorish castle, but also the *Palácio Nacional da Pena (April–Oct daily 9.45am–7pm | admission 14 euros | Nov–March daily 10am–6pm | admission 11.50 euros)*, a fairy-tale castle in the vein of Bavaria's Neuschwanstein, surrounded by a picturesque park. ☆ *Cruz Alta* (High Cross), the highest point of the Sintra hills (529 m/1735 ft), affords a unique panoramic vista. The castle itself, a romantic mix of Gothic, Baroque, Manueline, Renaissance and Moorish architecture, is accessible by taxi, by bus No. 434 or on foot. The walk through the INSIDER TIP fairy-tale woods takes about one hour. The Turismo has hiking maps, also for the new Vila Sassetti path up to the Moorish castle.

From Sintra, it is just under 15 km (9 miles) on the EN247 to *Cabo da Roca*, the rocky cape that forms the westernmost point of the European continent. ☆ The INSIDER TIP *Moninho Don Quixote windmill (Rua Campo da Bola 7 | Azoia)* converted into a terrace bar, shortly before the cape, could be the starting point or terminus of a spectacular coast walk. Information: *Turismo Sintra (tel. 2 19 23 11 57 | www.cm-sintra.pt)*

FIT IN THE CITY

A good running track leads from the transport hub of *Cais do Sodré* **(120 A6)** (*∅ L10*) 6 km (4 miles) to Belém along the Tagus, on the now beautifully laid-out Ribeira das Naus, where the explorers' ships used to be built, taking in sights such as the *Torre de Belém* and the Discoveries Monument. You know the excuses: it's too hot for sport, it's raining… Enough, you can go swimming whatever the weather. Lisbon's prettiest indoor swimming pool is located in an attractive district where you can swim a few lengths among locals. More information about the public opening times *(utilisação livre)* on the website: *Campo de Ourique indoor pool* **(132 C1)** (*∅ H8*) *(closed Aug | admission depending on the time of day 1.80–2.30 euros | Rua Correia Teles 103A | www.gcp.pt | bus 701 Prazeres | bus 742 Correia Teles)*

FOOD & DRINK

Traditional Portuguese cuisine is simple, rustic and hearty. Portions are usually generous. A hefty plate of fish or meat is complemented with rice and potatoes (often at the same time), plus a few lettuce leaves as standard garnish.

Sometimes you might find the unusual in the most simple of eateries *(tascas)*, where the *dona* of the house still cooks personally, lovingly following handed-down family recipes. Just look for places where the locals sit, talk and laugh!

Vegetarians used to be restricted in choice, often having to settle for an omelette with salad. Today, vegetarian and vegan food is sharply on the rise and you can find online information on vegetarian dining at *www.happycow. net* (type in *Lisbon*).

Lunch *(almoço)* is usually served between 1 and 3pm, while dinner *(jantar)* is served from about 8pm (though most diners arrive one hour later). To dine among locals, reserve a table for around 9pm and enjoy an aperitif beforehand on one of the city's delightful rooftop terraces. The appetisers appearing on the cover charge *(couvert)* such as olives, cheese, tuna pâté, bread and butter are charged.

The national dish is codfish, *bacalhau*, which the Portuguese like to call their faithful friend *(o fiel amigo)*. There are said to be at least 365 different ways to prepare it. Tasty, cheap and a popular favourite (fresh in the summer, otherwise frozen), grilled sardines *(sardinhas assadas)* are rubbed with coarse

Photo: Amêijoas à Bulhão Pato: mussels in a garlic and lemon sauce

The Atlantic is the larder of Portugal – take the chance while in town to taste the superb fresh fish and seafood dishes

sea salt and grilled over charcoal *(na brasa)*. Fans of shellfish *(mariscos)* will enjoy the *marisqueiras* (seafood restaurants). While the variety is impressive, do watch the (kilo) price. Lobster *(lavagante)* and crayfish *(lagostas)* aren't cheap in Lisbon either.

The Portuguese like their meat *(carne)* to be medium. Lamb *(borrego)* is a favourite choice. Another popular dish is crispy suckling pig *(leitão assado)*, which is offered in many basic eateries (e. g. among historic Azulejos at

the *Arena do Sabor (Rua Condes de Monsanto 4a | near Praça da Figueira)*. A speciality worth looking out for is *porco preto* from the Alentejo region south of Lisbon, an acorn-fed "black pig". If you like poultry, order the tasty grilled chicken *(frango assado)*, or for a spicier version, *piripiri*. The desserts *(sobremesas)* are good but often very sweet. Popular options include sweet rice *(arroz doce)*, caramel pudding *(pudim flan),* like a crème caramel, and milk custard *(leite creme)*. Make

Custard tarts straight from the oven: Unica Fábrica dos Pastéis de Belém

sure you try the specialities of Portugal's former colonies. Lisbon has many good Brazilian, Indian and African restaurants.

Wine lovers will have plenty of choice. Whether red *(vinho tinto)* or white wine *(vinho branco)*, there is always a good range available; Portugal has a profusion of native grape vines. A mid-range bottle *(garrafa)* ordered in a regular restaurant will cost about 12–16 euros. The house wine *(vinho da casa)* is even cheaper and usually pretty decent. The slighty bubbly summer wine *vinho verde* should only be enjoyed chilled *(bem fresco)*.

The latest food trends include healthy eating, creative fusion food, authentic Italian cuisine, *escabeche* and microbreweries. The half-day INSIDER TIP food tours organised by *Taste of Lisboa* (www.tasteoflisboa.com) offer excellent culinary insights into the Mouraria and Campo de Ourique districts. A professional as well as tasty experience served up with lots of insider know-how.

CAFÉS

ALCÔA (120 B4) *(⌘ M9)*

The icon of "monastic pastries" from Alcobaça opened a branch in Lisbon in 2017. Decorated with stunning tiles by ceramic artist Querubim Lapa, this shop's main ingredients are eggs and sugar, whipped up to create sublime Portuguese pastries such as "heaven's bacon", "cornucopias" and "egg chestnuts" as well as modern twists with caramel spirals and sprinkles of gold dust. It's standing room only here but you can devour the *pastéis* at the bar with a coffee. INSIDER TIP Its double mirror set in a tiled frame makes a great snapshot for Instagram or Facebook. *Daily 9am–10pm | Rua Garrett 37 | metro (blue, green) Baixa-Chiado*

CAFÉ A BRASILEIRA ●
(120 B4) (*M9*)

Lisbon's most famous café, the "Brazilian woman" owes its fame particularly to the poet Fernando Pessoa, who regularly drank his "juice" here (a glass of schnapps). In front of the café a bronze statue of the great man sitting at a table has pride of place. Inside, the atmosphere is agreeable, outside there's often a lot of loud street music. Late at night, night owls meet here to sip their espresso, the blinds are drawn only around 2am. *Rua Garrett 120 | metro (blue, green) Baixa-Chiado*

CAFÉ LINHA D'ÁGUA ★
(124 A5) (*K6*)

Above the Eduardo VII city park this laid-back cafeteria all in white with a pretty terrace is situated in the Amália Rodrigues garden, overlooking a small artificial lake. A studeny clientele (hardly any tourists) and self-service. WiFi. *Daily 10am–8pm | Rua Marquês da Fronteira | www.linhadeagua.pt | metro (blue) São Sebastião*

CAFÉ MARTINHO DA ARCADA
(121 D5) (*N10*)

Lisbon's oldest café was inaugurated in 1782. Again, Fernando Pessoa was a regular here, and would sometimes pay with poems. Portuguese cuisine is served – during the week, it's worth enquiring about cheaper *mini-pratos* that are served on the esplanada and in the cafetaria! *Praça do Comércio 3 | www.martinhodaarcada.pt | metro (blue, green) Baixa-Chiado*

CAFÉ TATI (134 C5) (*L10*)

Cakes, brunch and snacks all served in this cellar situated directly behind the market. Changing (music) events with a focus on jazz, Sun 6pm session. *Tue– Sun 11am–1am | Rua Ribeira Nova 36 | cafetati.blogspot.pt | metro (green) Cais do Sodré*

PÃO DE CANELA (134 B4) (*K–L9*)

This cosy café-restaurant with terrace has a faithful following. Artists, journalists, deputies from the nearby parliament and the bairro neighbours all enjoy the relaxed atmosphere under shady trees. *Daily | Praça das Flores 25–29 | bus 773 Praça das Flores.* And that's not all the Praça das Flores has to offer: it also houses a INSIDER TIP beer bar (*cerveteca* – order a round of *cervejas artesanal* for 9 euros), the trendy *Castro* restaurant and even an ⓥ organic pizzeria.

ÚNICA FÁBRICA PASTÉIS DE BELÉM
(130 C5) (*D11*)

Lisbon's most famous pastry has been manufactured here since 1837: *pastéis de Belém*, custard pies fresh from the oven. Don't be put off by the queues which are just for takeaways; you'll always find a table inside the labyrinth! And there's also a few tables in the courtyard. *Daily | Rua de Belém 84–92 |*

★ **Santo António**
Rub shoulders with artists and media folk in Alfama
→ p. 63

★ **Café Linha d'Água**
Relax among the lisboetas – after browsing through the department store next door
→ p. 59

★ **Pharmácia**
Fantastic view outside, authentic pharmacy decor inside → p. 61

MARCO POLO HIGHLIGHTS

near the Hieronymus Monastery | www. pasteisdebelem.pt | eléctrico 15 Bélem

RESTAURANTS: EXPENSIVE

BAIRRO DO AVILLEZ (120 A3) (*Ⓜ M9*)
José Avillez is the darling of Lisbon's food scene. A degustation menu paired with wine will set you back approx. 250 euros in his two-starred *Belcanto* restaurant at the Largo de S. Carlos. Alongside a more affordable establishment *(Cantinho do Aziz)* and an adjoining pizzeria in the Rua Duques de Bragança, this award-winning chef has now also set up his own gastronomic neighbourhood featuring snack bar, restaurant and gourmet shop. Although the taverna serving petiscos (tapas) wins in terms of visual appeal, his restaurant offers a better value for

money. A new addition is "Beco" (lane) which serves up an exclusive, aka expensive (100–130 euros without drinks), gourmet meal accompanied by cabaret. A delight for all the senses. *Daily noon–midnight | Rua Nova da Trindade 18 | tel. 2 15 83 02 90 | www.bairrodoavillez.pt*

RESTAURANTE 100 MANEIRAS
(120 A2) (*Ⓜ L9*)
At this trendy Bairro Alto restaurant, Bosnian star chef Ljubomir Stanisic serves up Portuguese-Mediterranean cuisine that would well merit a Michelin star. No à la carte, but superb tasting menus *(45 euros)*. There's also a bistro branch in nearby Chiado. If money is no object, choose the option offering matching Portuguese wines with each course *(plus 35 euros);* the white wines are particularly good. *Daily | Rua do*

FAVOURITE EATERIES

Surprises in the Mouraria Centre
Original, healthy snacks and soups are available at *Bruta Flor* **(121 D1)** (*Ⓜ N8*) *(Wed–Thu 3–11pm, Fri 3pm–midnight, Sat 11am–midnight, Sun 11am–11pm | Largo Maria Severa no. 7A/B | access via Rua do Capelão behind the Centro Comercial Mouraria | tel. 2 10 93 60 99 | Budget).* Delicious: the lemon and thyme cake and the mulled wine in winter. Vegan and vegetarian food, Ⓥ organic wines, temporary art exhibitions and occasional live music. Happy hour 6.30–8pm.

No microwave, no freezer – oh, là, là!
Creative, fresh, French-style Ⓥ organic cooking without a set menu: four main meals, two desserts for 28 euros; vegetarian dishes, organic wines. Where? In INSIDER TIP *Os Gazeteiros*

(121 F3) (*Ⓜ N9*) *(Tue–Wed 7–10pm, thu–Sat noon–2pm and 7.30–open end | Rua das Escolas Gerais 114/6 | tel. 2 18 86 03 99 | www.osgazeteiros.pt | eléctrico 28 Escola Gerais | Moderate)*

Japanese Portuguese
At *Infâme* **(135 D2)** (*Ⓜ N8*) *(Sun–Thu noon–3pm and 7–10.30pm, Fri/Sat until 11pm | Largo do Intendente/Pino Manique 6 | tel. 2 18 80 40 00 | www.1908lisboahotel.com | metro (green) Intendente | Moderate)*. Elegant atmosphere with high windows and subtle lighting, contemporary Portuguese food with Japanese influences. The presentation is first class (try the matcha green tea and litchi ice cream) and the service is friendly. The only drawback is the uninspiring house wine.

No reason to jump into the river at Atira-te ao Rio

Teixeira 35 | tel. 210990475 | www.restaurante100maneiras.com | metro (blue) Restauradores | metro (green) Rossio | then Elevador da Glória or on foot

RESTAURANTS: MODERATE

ATIRA-TE AO RIO (138 C4) (*M O*)
When the sun goes down over Lisbon, this is the place to be. The name of the restaurant in Cacilhas (Almada) on the other side of the Tagus translates as "Throw yourself into the River". Relax in one of the lounge chairs on the riverside terrace, admiring the view over the city. It is lovely in the afternoon as well. Too crowded? Maybe there's room in the neighbouring restaurant Ponto Final. *Tue–Thu noon–4pm, Fri/Sat noon–11pm, Sun noon–5pm | Cais do Ginjal 67–70 | tel. 212751380 | www.atirateaorio.pt | ferry from Cais do Sodré to Cacilhas, then about 15 min. on foot, turning right along the quay*

O DECADENTE (120 A2) (*M M9*)
Trendy Portuguese fusion cuisine. You can eat inside or "out" under plastic tarpaulin. Some vegetarian options. where INSIDER TIP If you come early (7pm), you have the chance to get one of the tables that can'tbe reserved. In fine weather, the bar next door *Insólito (www.theinsolito.pt)* with its amusing lift and great view is also worth a visit. Despite being slightly on the expensive side. *Daily, Sun brunch noon–4pm | Rua São Pedro de Alcântara 81 | tel. 213461381 | www.thedecadente.pt | metro (blue) Restauradores | then on foot or Elevador da Glória*

JESUS É GOÊS (134 C3) (*M M8*)
Small, brightly decorated bar attracting young people serving spicy hot specialities from the former Portuguese colony Goa. *Tue–Sun noon–3pm and 7–11pm | Rua de São José 23 | tel. 211545812 | metro (blue) Avenida or Restauradores*

PHARMÁCIA ★
(134 B5) (*M L9*)
Restaurant in the Pharmacy Museum building decorated in the museum's theme, serves unusual tapas, cocktails and a great surprise menu. A beautiful

LOCAL SPECIALITIES

açorda de marisco – bread stew with seafood (photo left)

amêijoas à bulhão pato – mussels in a garlic-lemon sauce

arroz de pato – rice with duck

bacalhau à brás – codfish potato gratin

bife à Marrare – fillet of beef in a garlic and cream sauce

bitoque – steak with fried egg and chips/fries

bolo-Rei – "King's Cake", traditional Christmas and Easter yeast cake made with dried fruit

cabrito – kid goat, prepared with fresh herbs

caldeirada à fragateira – fish stew with tomatoes and potatoes

caldo verde – soup made from kale and potatoes

cerveja – beer

chanfana – goat in wine sauce

cozido à portuguesa – hearty stew of various cuts of meat and vegetables

favas à moda de Lisboa – fava beans with bacon and sausage (photo right)

feijoada à portuguesa – bean stew with sausage

frango na púcara – chicken, prepared in a clay pot

iscas com elas – liver with spleen

lulas recheadas – stuffed squid, e.g. with chorizo and tomatoes

pão-de-ló – biscuit cake

pastéis de bacalhau – fried codfish pasties

pastéis de Belém/ pastéis de nata – puff pastry custard tarts

peixinhos da horta – fried green beans in tempura

porco à alentejana – pork goulash with mussels

queijadas de Sintra – sweet curd pastries from Sintra

rissóis de camarão – fried prawn rissoles

salada de polvo – octopus salad

lawn terrace enclosed with medicinal plants looks onto the *Miradouro de Santa Catarina*. *Tue–Sat 12.30pm–1am | Rua Marechal Saldanha 1 | tel. 2 13 46 21 46 | metro (blue, green) Baixa-Chiado*

RAMIRO (135 D3) *(Ⳮ N8)*
The atmosphere might not be the cosiest yet queues of people gather early in the evening outside this "seafood temple". INSIDER TIP Also very good, a few houses further on up the Avenida:

Marisqueira do Lis (no. 27b). *Tue–Sun noon–0.30am | Av. Almirante Reis 1H | tel. 218851024 | www.cervejariarami ro.pt | metro (green) Intendente*

SANTO ANTÓNIO ★ (121 F3) *(∅ N9)*

The restaurant next to the São Miguel church has a faithful following: film and media folk, as well as artists appreciate the Alfama ambience. In summer, a small romantic vine-covered terrace is an additional draw. International cuisine. *Daily | Beco de São Miguel 7 | tel. 218881328 | www.siteantonio.com | bus 28 Casa Conto | metro (blue) Santa Apolónia | then on foot*

TASCA KOME (121 D4) *(∅ N9)*

Stylish, cosy and authentic Japanese restaurant full of Japanese guests in Baixa serving visually perfect creations and specialities from Osaka. Sake cocktails and sushi, stuffed aubergines, salads, miso soups, matcha cake and lemonade. *Tue–Sat noon–3pm and 7–10.30pm | Rua Madalena 57 | tel. 211340117 | www. kome-lisboa.com | metro (blue) Terreiro do Paço*

RESTAURANTS: BUDGET

INSIDER TIP ▶ ASSOCIAÇÃO CABO-VERDEANA (134 B2) *(∅ L7)*

In its centre on the 8th floor, the community association of the Cape Verde Islands organises its trademark lunch dances on Tuesdays and Thursdays where guests can enjoy the national dish of Cachupa (a meat stew with beans and corn) before getting up for a dance. A "normal" lunch is served on the other days. *Mon–Fri noon–3pm | Rua Duque de Palmela 2 | tel. 213531932 | metro (blue, yellow) Marquês de Pombal*

CANTINA CHINESA (121 D1) *(∅ N8)*

Small, no-frills restaurant in Mouraria's Chinatown. All the food is freshly prepared; the ingredients are kept in Tupperware boxes in the cold counter waiting for you to pick what you'd like: bamboo, mushrooms, lotus, aubergines *(beringela),* excellent with pork *(carne de porco)* or vegetarian with soy sauce, spring onions and black beans – all for under 10 euros! The restaurant is known for its noodle soup and Chinese families

Meeting spot for creative people: the secluded terrace of Santo Antonio

like to eat here. The smoking ban is often ignored here. *Daily 10am—9pm | Calçada da Mouraria 7 | left up the steep road between Rua do Bemformoso and Rua do Cavaleiro*

CANTINHO LUSITANO (134 A4) (*🗺 K9*)
Delicious *petiscos* (tapas) and splendid wines in a very intimate one-room restaurant (reservation recommended!). Young, enthusiastic owners and a pleasant mix of clientele. *Tue–Sat 7pm–midnight | Rua dos Prazeres 52 | tel. 218 06 51 85 | www.cantinholusitano.com | metro (yellow) Rato | then 10 minutes on foot*

CASA DO ALENTEJO (120 B4) (*🗺 M8*)
The house representing the Alentejo region south of Lisbon is an architectural rarity with neo-Moorish details and tile decorations. Rustic dishes in the two halls upstairs and the small tasca with courtyard downstairs. Dancing on Sundays *(mid-Sept–May Sun 3–7pm, admission 5 euros). Daily | Rua Portas de Santo Antão 58 | tel. 213 40 51 40 | www.casadoalentejo.pt | metro (blue) Restauradores*

CHEMINÉS DO PALÁCIO – KANTINA (120 C2) (*🗺 M9*)
Daily specials from various regions in Portugal in the bordeaux-red Palace of Independence: The restoration of the Portuguese monarchy was planned in conspiracy here in the 17th century and the few surviving monarchists still have an office here. In summer, sit out in its pretty courtyard or eat inside under two chimneys, reminiscent of the National Residence in Sintra: Cheminés do Palácio. *Mon–Sat noon–3pm and 7–10pm | Largo de S. Domingos | tel. 213 42 03 91 | metro (green) Rossio*

INSIDER TIP ▶ A FABULOSA CAFETERIA DE SANTOS (134 B5) (*🗺 L10*)
A modern lunchtime hangout for locals is this fabulous café-restaurant housed in a former screw factory. An insider tip for during the week. Specialities of the house include the melt-in-the-mouth croquettes as well as uniquely-filled sandwiches, soups and salads (with chicken, avocado, parmesan etc.). The décor combines minimalistic white and dark-stained wood. The café also serves good breakfasts or *lanche* in the late afternoon. Around the corner, at Rua Boavista no. 186, is the splendid, photogenic shop front covered in yellow tiles which sells screws (the lettering says "parafusos"). *Mon–Fri 8.30am–7pm | Rua do Instituto Industrial 7h | metro (green) Cais do Sodré | bus 714 Conde de Barão | eléctrico 25 Conde de Barão*

LOW BUDGET

The best feature of the Catholic *A.C.I.S.J.F.* canteen, popularly known as "the nuns" *(as freiras)* **(120 B5)** (*🗺 M10*) *(Mon–Fri noon–3pm | Travessa do Ferragial 1 | tel. 2 13 24 09 10 | eléctrico 28 R. Vitor Cordon/R. Serpa Pinto)* is the terrace. A lunch (self-service) costs just 6.20 euros, snacks 1–2 euros.

Camaradas! The canteen in Portugal's Communist Party (PCP) headquarters serves a cheap lunchtime meal to visitors **(134 C3)** (*🗺 L8*) *(Mon–Fri noon–2pm | Av. da Liberdade 170 | tel. 2 13 30 70 00 | metro (blue) Restauradores)*: Main meal 2.50 euros! Soup 90 cents, fruit 50 cents.

Rustic tile art and hearty food: Casa do Alentejo

FLORESTA DAS ESCADINHAS
(121 D3) (*M–N9*)

This funnily named grill restaurant, "little forest on the little stairs", is only open for lunch but serves the city's best sardines. *Tue–Sat noon–4pm | Rua de Santa Justa 3 | tel. 2 18 87 20 52 | metro (green) Rossio*

INSIDER TIP FOOD TEMPLE
(121 D1) (*N8*)

Small vegetarian-vegan restaurant in Mouraria. The food is extremely cheap. Regularly alternating dishes. You can almost believe you are on a film set in summer. Reservation recommended. *Wed–Sun 7.30–11pm | Beco do Jasmim 18 | from the Rua da Mouraria, turn into Rua do Capelao at the guitar statue, then up to the right | tel. 2 18 87 43 97 | www.thefoodtemple.com | metro (green) M. Moniz*

A LAREIRA (135 F4) (*O9*)

Although there's no fireplace *(lareira)* and only three tiny tables, this establishment has everything a good restaurant should offer: delicious, affordable and authentic Portuguese food. The proprietors, Gracida and José, from the far north of Portugal don't speak English but will use their hands and feet to communicate with guests if they have to. The speciality is *novilho* (young bull meat). *Tue–Sun 9am–midnight | Rua do Paraiso 104 | tel. 2 18 87 28 67 | metro (blue) Santa Apolónia*

A NOVA POMBALINA (121 D4) (*∅ *)

Locals get their vitamin boost in this sandwich bar with its delicious freshly squeezed juices. Speciality: slow-roasted pork sandwich. *Mon–Sat 7.30am–7pm | Rua do Comércio 2 | metro (blue) Terreiro do Paço*

STASHA (120 A3) (*M9*)

Dependable option in Bairro Alto, a short distance from Largo Luis de Camões. Good vegetarian options, friendly service, open on Sundays. *Mon–Sat noon–3.30pm and 6.30–11.30pm, Sun 6.30–11.30pm | Rua das Gáveas 33 | tel. 2 13 43 11 31 | metro (blue, green) Baixa-Chiado*

SHOPPING

CITY **WHERE TO START?**
Most shops can be found in downtown **Baixa (120–121 C–D)** (*M–N 9–10*) (shoe stores!), in chic **Chiado (120 B4–5)** (*M9–10*), along the **Avenida da Liberdade** and the **Avenida da Roma**. The **Bairro Alto (120 A2–3)** (*L9*) (Upper Town) has many shops selling quirky fashion, music and eccentric living accessories – while often only opening from 11am/noon, they then stay open until late at night.

Charmingly nostalgic little shops seemingly untouched by modern times: in **Lisbon you'll still find them.** These traditional stores can often be recognised by the fact that their name and address is inlaid in the pavement outside in black cobblestones. These shops have nearly always been in the same family for generations, and the owners are masters of their profession. Hurry is unknown here. Even if you are only buying a button, choosing the right one can take a while. Once things are finally agreed, the item is wrapped up, *embrulhar* in Portuguese, with loving care.

True treasure troves for those with a bit of time on their hands are the tiny haberdashery shops along *Rua da Conceição* in the Baixa. Things move much faster in the major shopping centres. These modern temples to consumer-

Shopping is a real experience here – be it in old buildings or in ultra modern shopping centres

ism on the periphery of the city are much like those in other capital cities: fast food and *fast forward* is the order of the day here. While traditional shopping hours are 9am to 7pm with a one-hour break for lunch (1–2pm), the shopping centres are open until at least 11pm every day.

Typical products of Portugal are *azulejos* (tiles) and ceramic ware, embroidery, copper-, cork- and basket ware. Culinary specialities such as dried fruit, salt, honey, olives and wine make good souvenirs for friends and family. Another good buy is the high-quality olive oil *(azeite)*, sold on every corner. Leather goods are cheaper than in northern Europe, as is high-grade gold and silver jewellery. Shopaholics may like to invest in the so-called Eat & Shop Card (6 euros) from the tourist offices, which will entitle them to discounts in some 100 shops as well as at least 10 percent off in 30 participating restaurants. Information: *www.askmelisboa.com*

Shopping temple flooded with light:
Centro Comercial Vasco da Gama

ANTIQUES

Most antiques shops cluster around the *Rua Dom Pedro V.* and the *Rua de S. Bento*.

ANDRADE (120 A4) (*M10*)

Off the main antiques shops drag: art objects of the 17th and 18th centuries. *Rua do Alecrim 48/50 | metro (blue, green) Baixa-Chiado | www.jandrade-antiguidades.com*

BOOKSHOPS & ANTIQUARIANS

Bookshops cluster between the *Rua do Carmo* and the *Rua Nova do Almada* as well as in the *Bairro Alto*; the big FNAC retail chain (books, music, electronics) is located in the shopping centre *Armazéns do Chiado*.

FÁBULA URBIS ● (121 E4) (*N9*)

This well-stocked bookshop sells titles on Lisbon and Portugal as well as Portuguese cookbooks, travel books, novels etc. in all the major languages, and its knowledgeable staff can dispense advice. The top floor sometimes puts on exhibitions or free recitals. *Daily 10am–1.30, 3–8pm | Rua de Augusto Rosa 27 | www.fabula-urbis.pt | bus 37 | eléctrico 12, 28 Limoeiro*

SHOPPING CENTRES

AMOREIRAS SHOPPING CENTER ● (129 E4–5) (*J7*)

This 80s-postmodern high-rise complex with almost 300 shops, restaurants and cinemas is a major draw for Lisboetas, especially on Sundays. New: the ☀ Miradouro rooftop viewing platform (*5 euros | www.amoreiras360view.com*) with a panoramic view – great at sunset. *Daily 10am–11pm | Av. Engenheiro Duarte Pacheco | metro (yellow) Marquês de Pombal, Rato | bus 711 Armoeiras*

CENTRO COMERCIAL COLOMBO ● (138 C3) (*O*)

One of the biggest shopping centres in Europe! Shops, restaurants, cinemas and bowling – and it all comes at a price. Only the garden is free. *Daily 9am–midnight | Benfica | www.colombo.pt | metro (blue) Colégio Militar/Luz*

CENTRO COMERCIAL VASCO DA GAMA ★ (123 E3) (*R–S2*)

The modern shopping mall, in avantgarde design with lots of natural light, is situated right on the Parque das Nações.

It has an excellent selection of clothes stores (including a few Portuguese brands, e.g. at the Ericeira surf shop), a supermarket, ☆ terrace bars with river view, and cinemas. *Daily 9am–midnight | www.ccn trovascodagama.pt | metro (red) Oriente*

CRAFTS & SOUVENIRS

APAIXONARTE (134 B5) (*Ø K9*)

Urban Portuguese arts and crafts, surrealistic azulejos, unusual t-shirts, cool Japanese-style clutches, cartoon-style dolls – and art exhibitions from local artists. *Mon–Fri noon–7.30pm, Sat 10am–3pm | Rua Poiais de São Bento 57–59 | www.apaixonarte.com | eléctrico 28 Rua Poiais de São Bento | metro (green) Cais do Sodré*

INSIDERTIP▶ CAMILLA WATSON STUDIO (121 D2) (*Ø N9*)

This British photographer portrays the community of the old city: neighbours standing against the Beco das Farinhas house walls and fado greats in the lanes behind the Rua da Mouraria. Her *Canto do Sol* installation from 2017 on Rua dos Lagares (121 E1) (*Ø d2*) also showcases her work. Camilla's silver gelatine prints and mosaic tiles are special souvenirs to take back home. And don't forget to say hello to Dom Quixote, Camilla's Portuguese water dog! *Mon–Sat 10.30am–6.30pm (irregular) | Largo dos Trigueiros 16a | www.camillawatsonphotography.net | metro (green) Rossio*

CORK & CO (120 A 3–4) (*Ø L–M9*)

Original cork products, decorative objects, bags, jewellery and much more are on offer at this cool shop. *Mon–Sat 11am–8pm, in season also Sun 5–8pm | Rua das Salgadeiras 10 | www.corkand company.pt | metro (blue, green) Baixa-Chiado*

EPAL ♻ (134 C3) (*Ø M8*)

Lisbon's tap water is perfectly clean and safe to drink; a half-litre "fill forever bottle" can be bought from the vending machine in the entrance of the city's public water company. Available in seven different colours and a cool design, this refillable bottle makes an ideal "green souvenir" at a price of 1.50 euros. *Mon–Fri 8.30am–7.30pm | Av. da Liberdade 24 | www.epal.pt | metro (blue) Avenida*

A LOJA (121 D3) (*Ø N9*)

Photographer Gabrielle de Saint-Venant sells a fine selection of vintage objects and clothing, unusual Portuguese crafts, retro objets d'art and "frivolities". Great gifts: Soaps with an azulejo pattern or a muesli bowl with colourful sprinkles from the Alentejo region. An added bonus: information on the city's best

---

MARCO POLO HIGHLIGHTS

★ **Centro Comercial Vasco da Gama**
Architecturally impressive shopping centre → p. 68

★ **Fábrica Sant'Anna**
Azulejos, including tailor made on request → p. 70

★ **A Vida Portuguesa**
The ultimate shop for all fans of nostalgia and retro design → p. 70

★ **Feira da Ladra**
A flea market for browsing with lots of local colour → p. 70

★ **LX Market**
Cool clothing, arts and crafts and a spot of people watching on Sundays! → p. 71

places to visit. *Opening times vary | Largo São Cristóvão 3 | opposite the church | www.facebook.com/ALoja.Lisboa | metro (green) Rossio*

Ó! GALERIA (121 E1) (*M N8*)

Virtually every centimetre of wall space is covered with works from Portuguese illustrators in this gallery for graphics and prints. *Mon–Sat 11am–7pm, in the summer until 8pm | Calçada de Santo André 86 | www.ogaleria.com | metro (green) Martim Moniz*

RENOVA (121 D5) (*M N10*)

Sexiest WC on Earth: Go to the loo in style for just one euro and choose which one of the many different colours of toilet paper you want to use; the colourful toilet rolls (black especially) from the Portuguese company Renova are a design hit. If you're not in need, you can simply wander around the store for free. **INSIDER TIP** A great souvenir for back home are the serviettes with prints of Lisbon's attractions – famous city monuments, tram 28 etc. *Daily 9am–9pm | Terreiro do Paço/ under the arcades of the Praça do Comércio | www.myrenova.com | metro (blue) Terreiro do Paço*

FÁBRICA SANT'ANNA ★

One of the oldest ceramics and azulejo manufacturers in the city. Shop: *Rua do Alecrim 95* (120 A4) (*M M9–10*) *| metro (blue, green) Baixa-Chiado.* At the factory, visitors are allowed to watch production. Factory: *Mon–Fri 10am–12.30pm and 2–6pm | Calçada da Boa-Hora 96* (131 E4) (*M E11*) *| tel. 2 13 63 82 92 | www.santanna.com.pt | bus 732 Boa-Hora*

A VIDA PORTUGUESA ★
(120 B4) (*M M9*)

For everybody who loves to browse, in both shops of the "Portuguese life", you'll find a tasteful and colourful assortment of retro household products as well as stationery, cosmetics and foods such as olive oil tasting sets, port chocolate, tea from the Azores, Medronho strawberry tree vinegar, Flor de Sal and more. Everything is *made in Portugal*. The main store is in Chiado, the branch at the hip Intendente square (135 D2–3) (*M N8*), another one selling household items at Rua Ivens 2 (134 C5) (*M M10*). *Mon–Sat 10am–8pm, Sun 11am–8pm | Rua Anchieta 11 | www.avidaportuguesa.com | metro (blue, green) Baixa-Chiado*

LOW BUDGET

At the *Centro Comercial Mouraria* (121 D1) (*M N8*) *(Mon–Sat 9am–8pm | Praça Martim Moniz | metro (green) Martim Moniz)* Chinese, African and Indian vendors sell clothes, jewellery, household goods, exotic foods, some at wholesale prices. The small streets around the Centro Comercial shelter dozens of tiny shops and cheap restaurants.

Wines from Portugal with cheap tastings from machines at the *Wine Tasting Room* (120 C5) (*M M–N10*) *(March–Oct daily 11am–7pm, Nov–Feb Mon–Sat 11am–7pm | Praça do Comércio | www.viniportugal.pt | metro (blue, green) Baixa-Chiado*

MARKETS

FEIRA DA LADRA ★
(135 F3–4) (*M O8–9*)

Tuesdays and Saturdays (9am–4pm), the *Campo de Santa Clara,* to the left behind the church of *São Vicente,* hosts the *Feira da Ladra*, the "Market of the Thieving Woman" (it used to be the place to sell stolen goods). Today, it's a regular flea market selling a lot of things that might otherwise have landed on the tip. But don't get your hopes up too much:

MERCADO CAMPO DE OURIQUE
(129 D–E6) *(᷄ H–J8)*

The popular busy market has an excellent selection of fresh produce, especially fruit and veg, meat and fish. The *pastelaria* at the corner *(Rua Coelho da Rocha 99 | www.omelhorbolodechoco*

Hunting for bargains on the "Market of the Thieving Woman"

the professionals know exactly what to charge! Gastro pubs are popping up all around here: enjoy a leisurely INSIDER TIP milky coffee along with freshly filled focaccias and more at the Jardim de Santa Clara. *Eléctrico 28 Voz Operário*

LX MARKET ★ (132 B4) *(᷄ G10)*

First and second-hand clothing, urban crafts and antiques – the LX Market is where hipsters come to find them. This Sunday market is the perfect place to explore the inside and outside of the *LX Factory (see p. 80)* buy a unique "made-in-Lisbon" item and do a spot of people watching. *Sun 10am–6pm | Rua Rodrigues de Fária 103 | LX Factory | www.lxmarket.com | eléctrico 15 Calvário | bus 714 Calvário*

latedomundo.com) claims to make the "best chocolate cake in the world", with either dark or milk chocolate. Can ideally be combined with a visit to the *Casa Fernando Pessoa (see p. 24). Sun–Thu 10am–11pm, Fri/Sat 10am–1am | Rua Coelho da Rocha | eléctrico 25, 28 Rua Saraiva Carvalho | bus 709 Saraiva Carvalho*

TIME OUT MERCADO DA RIBEIRA ●
(134 B–C6) *(᷄ L10)*

This spacious, restored market hall built in 1902 shows neo-Moorish influences. Today the local city magazine has rebranded many of these traditional market stalls selling fruit and vegetables with the status of being (top) city restaurants. The lisboetas love tasting their way through the latest food trends served on the long tables; Marlene Vieira's stall with changing daily specials is a good go-to place. By the way, you can also buy food, tinned foods, jams, chocolate cake to take away! It has a quieter seating area outside. The market is gradually expanding into an all-round culinary and entertainment experience with the *Rive Rouge Club (www.rive-rouge.com)*, a venue for Lisbon locals to come and dance after work. *Sun–Wed 10am–midnight, Thu–Sat 10am–2am, market Mon–Sat 6am–2pm | Av. 24 de Julho | www.timeout.com | metro (green) Cais do Sodré*

FASHION & ACCESSORIES

The main shopping areas are the *Baixa* and the more upmarket *Chiado*, increasingly *Príncipe Real* with its concept stores. International designers have set up shop mainly along *Avenida da Liberdade*, while club and streetwear can be found in the *Bairro Alto.* Information on the Portuguese top designers: *www.modalisboa.pt*

A FÁBRICA DOS CHAPEUS
(134 C4) (*L9*)

Hats off to this designer store selling unique made in Lisbon models ranging from traditional flat caps, wide-brimmed straw hats and crushable cotton hats to turbans and wraparounds. If hats don't appeal to you, there are other quirky shops to explore in this street. *Mon–Thu 11am–8.30pm, Fri/Sat 11.30am–9pm | Rua da Rosa 118 | www.afabricadoschapeus.com | metro (blue, green) Baixa-Chiado*

FLY LONDON (134 B2) (*L8*)

Fly London's comfortable wedge shoes, attracting international followers, are useful for pounding Lisbon's steep pavements – the death of many a kitten heel

Traditional company behind the noble façade: Tailor-made gloves from Luvaria Ulísses

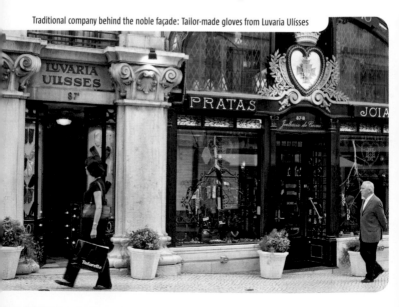

– in style. Flagship store. *Av. da Liberdade 230 | www. flylondon.com | metro (blue) Avenida*

JOSÉ ANTÓNIO TENENTE
(120 B3) (*M9*)

In a way, Tenente is Portugal's Escada. The versatile designer has two signature fashion lines – classics and jeans – but also makes bags, pens, glasses and even skiwear. *Travessa do Carmo 8 | www.jose antoniotenente.com | metro (blue, green) Baixa-Chiado*

LOJA DA BUREL
(120 B4) (*M9*)

Once a clothing item of shepherds, Burel, thick Portuguese black wool, has been resurrected by this company to create brightly coloured tops in original designs, with original cuts, cosy jackets, rucksacks with cleverly integrated hoods and pockets. Certainly not cheap, but all items are produced in the Portuguese mountains and are designed to last a lifetime. Edible souvenirs are also available – how about nettle pesto or apple and ginger vinaigrette in fun tubes? *Daily 10am– 8pm | Rua Serpa Pinto 15B | www.burel factory.com | metro (blue, green) Baixa-Chiado*

LUVARIA ULÍSSES (120 B3) (*M9*)
You have to visit this Lilliput store! Have a pair of colourful soft-to-the-touch leather gloves handmade to your size. *Rua do Carmo 87 | www.luvariaulisses.com | metro (green) Rossio*

JEWELLERY

ALTMANN-ZUZARTE (135 E4) (*N9*)
Roland Altmann makes jewellery, mainly from amber but also rings in Portuguese opal, quartz and even from 155 million year old dinosaur bones found in the Peniche region! Wear Jurassic Park on your finger with these stunning rings, the absolute eye catcher (approx. 100 euros). *Tue–Fri 2–7pm, Sat 10.30am– 1pm | Rua Senhora do Monte 1d | www. altmann-zuzarte.com | metro (green) Martim Moniz*

LINHA AÉREA (120 B3) (*M9*)
This is a treasure trove for style-conscious accessories junkies with small budgets. Costume jewellery, retro sunglasses, hair clips from the 1940s, toe rings and piercings are all here. *Corner shop behind Rossio/corner Rua do Carmo, Rua 1º Dezembro 3 | metro (green) Rossio*

WINE & OLIVE OIL

NAPOLEÃO (121 D4) (*N9*)
There are several wine shops to be found in Baixa. This is a firm favourite with its friendly staff who can speak several languages and are extremely knowledgeable. You can pop in to simply taste a glass – and get answers to questions such as what is green in the Vinho Verde? Good selection of popular wines in small bottles to taste. The remains of a Roman fish sauce production under the shop can also be seen. *Mon–Sat 9.30am–8pm | Rua Fanqueiros 70 | www.napoleao.co.pt | metro (blue, green) Baixa-Chiado*

OLISTORI (121 D3) (*N9*)
Recently opened temple for Portuguese extra virgin oils from all over the country. Ask for a INSIDER TIP free tasting! The store sells miniature bottle sets for you to take home as a souvenir. Their chocolate-covered olives are irresistible. *Mon–Sat 10.30am–8pm, in season also on Sundays | Rua da Madalena 137 | Facebook| metro (blue, green) Baixa-Chiado, after that Elevador do Castelo*

ENTERTAINMENT

CITY WHERE TO START?

The city's party mile is the **Bairro Alto (120 A2–3)** *(M L9)*. Later at night, the action moves to **Cais do Sodré (120 A5–6)** *(M L–M10)* on the Tagus shore, and further west to the **Docas** (docks) **de Alcântara** and **de Santo Amaro**. Much of **Santos (133 E–F 3–4)** *(M K9–10)*, around Avenida D. Carlos I, is given over to the teen scene, with cheaper restaurants, bars and clubs.

The Portuguese capital has something for everybody: intimate fado places, live music bars with African or Brazilian rhythms, cosy pubs, chic bars and clubs.

The party only gets started around 9.30pm in the bar district of *Bairro Alto* where locals hop from bar to bar, meeting old friends and new ones. The port district of *Cais do Sodré* is the 2am late-night party central. The action centres round *Rua Nova de Carvalho*, known locally as "Pink Street" – because of the colour of the tarmac – with its quirky restaurants. There is also a hub of activity around *Largo São Paulo*.

The fresh pastries baked by the **INSIDER TIP** *Padaria São Roque* (bakery) in *Rua da Rosa 186,* which starts work around 1am, sell like the proverbial hot cakes. An hour later, the exodus starts downhill to the *Cais do Sodré*, in the direction of Santa Apolónia train station to the hip club *Lux*, the *Avenida 24 Julho* or the

Night owls will be in heaven here: on the Tagus, entertainment starts late and offers far more than fado

Docas (*Doca de Santo Amaro* and *Doca de Alcântara*), a rather touristy open-air strip of restaurants and bars that also sees some daytime traffic on account of its riverside location. At weekends and on evenings preceding public holidays, the main nightlife areas are connected by free shuttle buses (Night Bus).

Major rock and pop concerts and opera are staged at the *Coliseu* (*Rua das Portas de Santo Antão 96 | www.coliseulisboa. com*) and the *MEO Arena* (*www.arena meo.pt*) at Parque das Nações. For an overview of what's on, consult the multilingual *Follow me* brochure or the Portuguese *Agenda LX,* also online. Tickets for all events can be bought at the *ABEP* kiosk at Restauradores, at *Fnac* in the Chiado shopping centre and online: *www.ticketline.pt.*

BARS

BICAENSE (134 B–C5) (*L9*)
This small bar/club hugging the rails of the *Elevador da Bica* is a favourite

with Lisbon's young art scene. It puts on occasional concerts and exhibitions, and has a very popular jazz session on Wednesdays. *Tue–Sat 7pm–2am | Rua Bica Duarte Belo 42 | eléctrico 28 Calhariz (Bica) | metro (blue, green) Baixa-Chiado*

A lot of old junk: Pavilhão Chinês

CASA INDEPENDENTE
(135 D2) (*∅ N8*)

INSIDER TIP *Largo do Intendente* was once a square infamous for drug-trafficking and prostitution. The square has undergone a successful revamp, a good example being this café-bar cultural centre. The entrance is slightly hidden from view with stairs leading up to alternative vibes and a plant-filled back patio. Homemade juices are available. Neighbours are the amiable *Josefina-Café-Restaurant*, an installation by pop artist Joana Vasconce-

los and the former azulejo factory, *Viúva Lamego*, with its photogenic façade. *Tue–Fri 2–11pm, Sat 2pm–2am | Largo do Intendente 45 | www.casaindependente. com | metro (green) Intendente*

GRAÇA DO VINHO (121 E2) (*∅ N9*)

Small and intimate wine bar which attracts locals. The wines are "shlent" (that's how the Portuguese pronounce *excelente*). The wine of the week costs 2.50 euros and pairs excellently with one of the cheeses on display in the counter – try the aromatic, melting *azeitão*. Salads are also served. *Mon–Fri 11am–midnight, Sat 11am–0.30am | Calçada da Graça 10 A/B | tel. 2 10 11 80 41 | Facebook | eléctrico 28 Largo da Graça | bus 734 Largo da Graça*

INSIDER TIP LX BREWERY
(125 D5) (*∅ M5–6*)

This microbrewery in Estefania serves up the latest craft beer creations, from rye ale to chocolate beer. You can order five 0.1-litre beers for 5 euros, a price you can't grumble about. The colourful bottle labels are printed with famous Lisbon sights. Snacks, table football and live viewing of sporting events. New: the *beer walk* to the city's brewing temples (40 well-invested euros) and *beer dinners*. *Mon–Thu 9am–7pm, Fri 9am–2am, Sat 9.30am–2am | Rua Funchal 5/Rua Ilha Terceira 42D | www.lxbeer.com | metro (yellow, red) Saldanha (Arco do Cego exit, then a few minutes on foot)*

PARK ✻ (134 B5) (*∅ L9*)

Typically Lisbon: There are no signposts to this trendy rooftop garden terrace on the 7th floor of the notorious local municipal parking company building EMEL on the edge of Bairro Alto. The menu includes hamburgers, cocktails and excellent coffee as well as live DJs on Thursdays to Saturdays. The main attraction is the view. The lift is sometimes out of order which means visitors use the adjacent spiral staircase. *Tue–Sat 1pm–2am, Sun 1–8pm | Calçada do Combro 58 | Facebook: Park Lisboa | metro (blue, green) Baixa-Chiado*

PAVILHÃO CHINÊS ★ (134 B4) (*ω L8*)

Bar museum and billiards salon. Bric-a-brac, kitsch and collectibles line every inch of the walls. Tea, cakes and snacks are served as well as alcohol. It's a must for all fans of vintage, but not cheap. *Mon–Sat 6pm–2am, Sun 9pm–2am | Rua Dom Pedro V 89 | Facebook | bus 78 Príncipe Real*

INSIDER TIP TEATRO DA GARAGEM (TABORDA) (121 E2) (*ω M8*)

One of these insider tips which you almost don't want to share with others: This unassuming, relaxing bar in the Theatre Taborda with tables made from wooden doors, a gallery full of lamps and fabulous views is never overcrowded. Snacks, salads, cakes... perfect for a romantic aperitivo. *Mon 6pm–midnight, Tue–Thu 3pm–midnight, Fri/Sat 3pm–2am, Sun 3pm–midnight | Rua da Costa do Castelo 75 | www.teatrodagaragem.com | eléctrico 12, 28*

TOPO ≈ (135 D4) (*ω M9*)

Trendy rooftop bar on the 6th floor of a former warehouse with panoramic views over the city and DJs. Blankets on cooler days, or there is space (and a restaurant) inside. *Mon–Wed, Sun 12.30pm–midnight, Thu–Sat 12.30pm–2am | Centro Comercial Martim Moniz/Largo Martim Moniz | on the side with the city wall remains | Facebook | metro (green) Martim Moniz*

CLUBS

The best information for clubbers: *www.viralagenda.com*

B.LEZA ★ (134 B6) (*ω L10*)

In the pink building on the river, the African community dances to intimately entwined Kizomba, Zouk & more. Live music and DJ, friendly atmosphere; women are asked to dance straightforwardly; men should test the waters so as not to drop a brick. The smoking ban is not taken too seriously. Best day: Fri. INSIDER TIP Sun (6pm) workshop Kizomba/Tarraxinha, live music from 8pm. *Thu-Sun 10.30pm–4am, Sun 6pm–4am | 10 euros minimum consumption | Rua Cintura do Porto de Lisboa 50 | Facebook | metro (green) Cais do Sodré*

BROWNIE (134 A3) (*ω K8*)

Small, exclusive bar/club. The proprietors describe it as a "fitness studio for avantgarde music – contemporary electronics and exercises in style" – in the trendy district of Príncipe Real. Don't be deterred by the run-down looking entrance and discreet sign – just knock on the door. Laid-back atmosphere. Gin & tonic cock-

---

★ Pavilhão Chinês
For lovers of all things retro-kitsch → **p. 77**

★ Lux
Still the undisputed meeting point for hipsters → **p. 78**

★ Mesa de Frades
Fado, surrounded by top-to-bottom azulejos → **p. 79**

★ Musicbox
Concerts from avantgarde to mainstream → **p. 81**

★ B.Leza
Creole sounds and sympathy → **p. 77**

MARCO POLO HIGHLIGHTS

For those lucky enough to get past the bouncers: Lux, the city's trendiest club

tails are the speciality. *Thu–Sat 11pm–4am | Rua da Imprensa Nacional 46 | tel. 9 66 72 01 01 | Facebook | metro (yellow) Rato | bus 758 Rua da Escola Politécnica*

INCÓGNITO (133 F3) (*꘠ K9*)

Timelessly trendy, this small club serves excellent indie, rock and Britpop. *Wed–Sat 11pm–4am | Rua Poiais de São Bento 37 | Facebook*

LUX ★ ☆ (136 C6) (*꘠ P9*)

The coolest club in town maintains its position as the hipsters' choice. The co-owner of this temple of dance is actor John Malkovich. While conversations are just about possible in the extensive first-floor lounge, in the basement the beat doesn't go much below 120 *beats per minute*. The cherry on the cake is the huge roof terrace with its great views over the Old Town and the Tagus. Up-and-coming dance bands often play gigs here, on Thursdays in particular, but also on Mondays. Expect long queues at weekends, when there's door policy from 2am. *Thu–Sat 11pm–6am | Av. Infante Dom Henrique 6f | Cais da Pedra opposite Santa Apolónia railway station | www.lux fragil.com | metro (blue) Santa Apolónia*

TITANIC SUR MER (134 B6) (*꘠ K8*)

New, alternative hotspot for live music, cabaret and underground events in a former fish auction house; an unpretentious venue serving cheap drinks where smoking is permitted. Jazz jam sessions on Mondays with free admission, **INSIDER TIP** Wed: Roda do Choro for fans of the Brazilian style of music and dance, Forró; the band (all dressed in suits!) is an institution in Lisbon. *Mon 10pm–2am, Wed/Thu (only when events) 11pm–6am, Fri/Sat 11pm–6am | Cais da Ribeira Nova /Cais do Sodré | Facebook | metro (green) Cais do Sodré*

TRUMPS (134 A3) (*꘠ K8*)

Classic disco on Lisbon's gay scene, yet hetero-friendly too. Its drag show has even veterans blushing. In the Principe Real neighbourhood, the heart of the gay community. *Fri/Sat 11.40pm–6am | Rua* da Imprensa Nacional 104b | tel. 9 15 93 82 66 | www.trumps.pt | metro (yellow) Rato

FADO

● Many fado venues today cater primarily to tourists, offering professional fado. Finding pure fado is really a matter of luck. Usually there is no entrance charge, but food and drink are considerably more expensive than in regular restaurants. Those arriving late (from 11pm at the earliest) can escape the otherwise obligatory meal. A bottle of wine costs at least 20 euros, a meal around 45 euros per person. Look out for signs announcing *fado vadio*: amateur fado, where anybody can have a go.

Authentic fado is difficult to track down simply because of the music's spontaneity. One trick is to go by night. When most tourists are heading back to their hotels for the night, the INSIDERTIP *Fado Night Tour (Wed–Sat 10pm–12.30am | from 20 euros (drinks not included), bookings have to be made before 4pm on the day of the tour | www.fadonighttour.com)* is only just setting out, taking guests to three different fado venues in Alfama; the meeting point is at the *Museu do Fado* (see p. 33). Tip: when the weather is fine, the fado legend Amália Rodrigues *(www.amaliarodrigues.pt)* often holds concerts in the museum's tapas garden restaurant.

INSIDERTIP MARIA DA MOURARIA
(121 D1) *(𝕞 N8)*

Fado bar run by Helder Moutinho (brother of the famous Camané) situated in the very house where the legendary 19th century *fadista* Maria da Sevéra lived and also tragically died at an early age. *Wed–Sun 5pm–2am | Largo da Severa 2 | Rua do Capelão: from the Rua da Mouraria up the street with the guitar statue | www.mariadamouraria.pt*

MESA DE FRADES ★ (135 F4) *(𝕞 O9)*

You'll be mingling with the younger generation at this beautiful fado tavern in a former chapel decked out with tiles. The fado usually doesn't start before 11pm. Reservation recommended. *Closed Tue | Rua dos Remédios 139a | tel. 9 17 02 94 36 | Facebook | metro (blue) Santa Apolónia*

A NINI (129 F3) *(𝕞 K6)*

At Nini's INSIDERTIP regular fado sessions on a Thursday night, authentic and friendly. *Thu from 9pm, fado from around 11pm (booking advised) | Rua Dom Francisco Manuel de Melo 36a | tel. 2 13 87 00 41 | bus 12 Artilharia Um/Rua D. Francisco M. Melo*

CINEMAS

Foreign films are shown in the original version with Portuguese subtitles. Current blockbusters are screened in the shopping centre cinemas. Schedules on *www.cinecartaz.publico.pt*. The *Cinemateca (Rua Barata Salgueiro 39 | www.cinemateca.pt)* shows Arthouse films.

ARTS CENTRES

CENTRO CULTURAL DE BELÉM
(130 B5) *(𝕞 C12)*

Classical, jazz, pop, rock and ethno music, ballet, modern dance and exhibitions. ● Joe Berardo exhibits his collection of contemporary art for free over two of the building's floors. Nice cafetaria.*Tel. 2 13 61 24 40 | www.ccb.pt | train Cais do Sodré, eléctrico 15 Centro Cultural de Belém*

FÁBRICA BRAÇO DA PRATA
(127 E4) *(𝕞 O)*

It's worth heading to this former ammunition factory to the east of Lisbon at weekends: Rub shoulders with the locals at the organised dance events and workshops, exhibitions and other cultural events. Cheap admission and tasty food. To get back to the city: the 781 bus runs every hour or take a taxi from the taxi stand 50m away or get the bar staff to call one. *Wed/Thu 7pm–2am, Fri/Sat 6pm–4am | Rua da Fábrica de Material de Guerra 1 | www.bracodaprata.com | buses 718, 728 Poço Bispo*

LX FACTORY ● (132 B4) (⫘ G10)
This hip arts complex occupies a former textile factory. The cool *Ler devagar* bookshop-cum-café *(www.lerdevagar. com)* has books up to the ceiling, holds experimental concerts and stays open until 2am on weekends. A current hotspot is the INSIDER TIP rooftop terrace Rio Maravilha *(www.riomaravilha.pt)*. Also clubs, artists' studios, restaurants (serving a variety of cuisine from pizza, moules & frites and Malaysian food to brunch). A cool neighbour (reached by crossing the CARRIS museum site

and walking 200 m (650 ft) along the tram tracks) is the INSIDER TIP *Village Underground:* a co-working space in out-of-service double-decker buses and containers with café-restaurant, DJs and events. Best visited between Tue and Fri. *Daily, varying opening times | Rua Rodrigues Faria 103 | tel. 2 13 14 33 99 | www. lxfactory.com | eléctrico 15, 18 Largo do Calvário*

INSIDER TIP MOURADIA
(121 D2) (⫘ N9)
An exciting, slightly hidden meeting place for young, alternative-minded tourists is the central office of the neighbourhood organisation "Renovar a Mouraria" with its casual snack bar, the takings of which are donated to the urban revival of this district. Guided tours, language courses, free concerts, cooking lessons from international inhabitants, film evenings and much more besides fill up the agenda. *Tue–Sat noon–midnight | Beco do Rosendo 8 | metro (green) Rossio*

LOW BUDGET

Lisbon's nightlife is not only vibrant, it's cheap too. A small beer on a *Bairro Alto* street might set you back as little as 1 euro; a half-litre "bucket" of caipirinha about a fiver.

To ensure that the clubs are full on weekdays as well as weekends, women get free drinks in a number of places. Ladies' nights are very popular with the gentlemen too. *Tue at Dock's (Doca da Alcântara) | Wed at the 80s club Plateau (133 E4) (⫘ K10) (Escadinhas da Praia 7 | Santos) and at the W (132 B5) (⫘ G10) (Rua Maria Luísa Holstein 13).*

MUSIC CLUBS & LIVE EVENTS

GALERIA ZÉ DOS BOIS
(120 A3) (⫘ L9)
An institution in the city's cultural life. Everybody has played in this former city palace, from local Blues icons such as Legendary Tigerman and guitarist Lobo to international guests as well as psychedelic afro sounds and improvisations. Exhibitions (Wed–Sat from 6pm). *Varying opening times, concerts usually from 10pm | Rua da Barroca 59 | www.zedosbois.org | metro (blue, green) Baixa-Chiado*

HOT CLUBE (134 C3) (⫘ L8)
Top meeting point for jazz lovers. Tue jam sessions. *10pm–2am, closed Sun–Mon | Praça da Alegria 39 | www.hcp.pt | metro (yellow) Avenida*

A temple of Portuguese music: Teatro Politeama

LOUNGE (134 B5) (*M L10*)

Casual bar, casual crowd, variety of music and concerts with free admission! Extremely smoky! *Closed Mon | Rua da Moeda 1 | opposite the lower entrance of Elevador da Bica | Facebook: Lounge Bar Lisboa | eléctrico 25 Rua S. Paulo (Bica) | metro (green) Cais do Sodré*

MUSICBOX ★ (120 A5) (*M M10*)

This tunnel-like club is a fixture for all fans of house, electro pop and alternative sounds. Nothing happens here before 2am unless it's a concert day. *Tue–Thu, Sun 10pm–6am, Fr/Sat 11pm–6am | Rua Nova de Carvalho 24 | www.musicboxlisboa.com | metro (green) Cais do Sodré*

THEATRE, MUSICAL & OPERA

Lisbon's long-established theatres, such as *São Luíz* and *Trindade* in Chiado and *Dona Maria II* on Rossio, are beautiful to behold, but performances are in Portuguese only. The *Teatro Nacional São Carlos* opera mostly puts on Italian works.

The Gulbenkian Foundation (*www.musica. gulbenkian.pt*) has its own concert halls and orchestra playing an international program with **INSIDER TIP** free admission on the first Sunday of the month (4 pm) at the museum building. *Tickets: 10–60 euros.*

TEATRO CAMÕES (123 F4) (*M S3*)

Home of the national ballet troupe *Companhia Nacional de Bailado (CNB)*, also visiting ballet companies. *Parque das Nações | Passeio do Neptuno | tel. 218 92 34 77 | www.cnb.pt | metro (red) Oriente*

TEATRO POLITEAMA (120 B1) (*M M8*)

Theatre in a 1920s style where in-house director Filipe La Féria puts on all manner of successful musicals – international musicals Portuguese-style and Portuguese originals such as a musical about fado queen Amália Rodrigues. *Tue–Sat 9.30pm, Sat/Sun also 5pm | Rua das Portas de Santo Antão 109 | tel. 213 40 57 00 | www.teatro-politeama. com | metro (blue) Restauradores*

WHERE TO STAY

Those looking for accommodation in Lisbon have never been so spoilt for choice. The hotel industry is prospering, occupancy rates are high and the construction sector is booming.

Compared to other European capitals, hotels in Lisbon are low-priced. A tourist tax of one euro a day has however been charged since 2016 (up to 7 days) which is payable when checking out. They are classified into five categories, following international standards. Most of the international chains are in the side streets and avenidas around the *Praça Marquês de Pombal.* Relatively cheap accommodation is available in pensions *(pensão),* residences *(residencial),* apartments and cool guesthouses. The online site for holiday homes *(www.airbnb.com)*

is extremely well established in the city. A phenomenon in Lisbon is the many backpacker hostels that have come in on the back of the low-budget flights. Lisbon has held the title of the world's best hostel city for several years and even the most reserved travellers can meet people thanks to the range of activities on offer (best example: the exclusive hostel Independente, *www. theindependente.pt).* Award-winning establishments are *Home Lisbon Hostel* (see p. 88) and *Lisbon Lounge (www. lisbonloungehostel.com).* The author's favourite: INSIDER TIP *Inn Possible (Rua Regedor 3 | www.innpossiblelisbon. com)* in Mouraria. Twin rooms with two separate beds are usually larger and a bit more expensive than double rooms

Prince or princess for a night!
Find accomodation in one of the city's ancient
palaces or former factories

(duplo). A single room is a *quarto individual*.

HOTELS: EXPENSIVE

BAIRRO ALTO HOTEL ✲
(120 A4) *(⫿ M9)*

Luxury with Old Town character: staying at this small five-star boutique hotel you'll feel like a true Lisboeta, right in the heart of the hustle and bustle, but with all the comforts and service of a top hotel. The unbeatable terrace bar is open to non-residents *(in summer daily 12.30pm–1am). 55 rooms | Praça Luis de Camões 2 | tel. 2 13 40 82 88 | www.bairroaltohotel. com | metro (blue, green) Baixa-Chiado*

HOTEL BRITÂNIA (134 C2) *(⫿ L8)*

Art-deco gem, generous rooms with plenty of atmosphere. Marble baths, formal service. The only downside is its view onto an office block. *32 rooms | Rua Rodrigues Sampaio 17 | tel. 2 13 15 50 16 | www.hotel-britania.com | metro (blue) Avenida*

And what to do after all the sightseeing? Head to the Memmo Alfama rooftop terrace

INTERNACIONAL DESIGN HOTEL
(120 C3) (*M9*)

This hotel with its pretty purple-and-white Belle Époque façade is situated right on Rossio. Each floor has a trendy design theme: Zen, Pop, Urban, and Tribal. Room sizes range from small to extra-large. Asia-inspired restaurant, good service, wine bar. *55 rooms | Rua da Betesga 3 | tel. 21324 09 90 | www.idesignhotel.com | metro (green) Rossio*

LISBOA PLAZA (134 C3) (*L8*)

Centrally located hotel, pretty, cosy and with plenty of atmosphere. *94 rooms, 12 suites | Travessa Salitre 7/Av. da Liberdade | tel. 213 21 82 18 | www.lisbonplazahotel.com | metro (blue) Avenida*

MEMMO ALFAMA ★ (121 E4) (*N9*)

Once a bakery and a shoe factory, this converted four-star hotel has been designed to make its guests feel at home. Decorated in subtle, modern colours, the rooms are small, a feature which is more than compensated for by their splendid terraces with mini pools. And what is more: INSIDER TIP hotel guests can join in a free guided tour of the district every morning at 10 am. *42 rooms| Travessa das Merceeiras 27 | tel. 210 49 56 60 | www.memmohotels.com | eléctrico 12, 28 Limoeiro*

MEMMO PRÍNCIPE REAL
(134 B–C 3–4) (*O*)

This hotel packs a statement in its white cube building. It is located on the main artery through the trendy district of Príncipe Real, albeit slightly away from the main road. The younger brother of the Memmo Alfama is just a stone's throw from Bairro Alto and only a bit further from Chiado. Spacious rooms, ☆ most of which offer splendid views. *41 rooms | Rua Dom Pedro 56 | tel. 219 01 68 00 | www.memmohotels.com | bus 758 Príncipe Real*

PALACETE CHAFARIZ D'EL REI
(121 F4) (𝄞 N9)

Alfama Palace with an abundance of style (Neo-Moorish, Art Déco), a panoramic ☀ balcony with Tagus views and personal service. As the hotel is hard to find, we recommend taking the chauffeur service from the airport. *6 suites | Travessa do Chafariz d'el Rei | tel. 218 88 61 50 | www.chararizdelrei.com | metro (blue) Terreiro do Paço or Santa Apolónia*

PALACIO RAMALHETE ★
(133 E4) (𝄞 J10)

This 17th century palace was converted into a boutique hotel. Stylish rooms and suites full of individual character, fantastic pool terrace. *12 rooms | Rua das Janelas Verdes 92 | tel. 213 93 13 80 | www.palacio-ramalhete.com | eléctrico 15 Cais da Rocha | bus 714 Ruas das Janelas Verdes*

SANTIAGO ALFAMA (121 E3) (𝄞 N9)

Five-starred accommodation run by a Dutch-Portuguese couple in a delightfully restored 15th-century palace: It's cosy with warm woods and pastel blue, aquamarine and beige tones. Friendly staff, welcome port wine and scones. You feel transported to the heart of Alfama in the hotel's airy breakfast room. ☀ Some of the cheaper rooms also offer excellent views; it's worth inquiring if they are free. Exquisite details, from a staircase of Roman steps to a vertical courtyard garden. INSIDER TIP Paying guests receive a 10% discount for The Mill – a trendy mixture of coffee shop and wine bar. *19 rooms | Rua de Santiago 10–14 | tel. 213 94 16 16 | www.santiagodealfama.com*

SOLAR DO CASTELO ★
(121 E2) (𝄞 N9)

This delightful, cosy hotel nestles within the walls of the Castelo de São Jorge.

The 18th-century palace has been tastefully restored, and the buffet breakfast is taken in the attractive courtyard. *14 rooms | Rua das Cozinhas 2 | tel. 218 80 60 50 | www.solardocastelo.com | bus 37 Castelo | eléctrico 12 Castelo*

HOTELS: MODERATE & GUESTHOUSES

1908 (135 D2) (𝄞 N8)

One of the most important hotels to open in 2017. The neo-Baroque building with colourful Art Nouveau floral features dates back to 1908 when it was awarded the Valmor prize for architecture. In those days, the buzzing artery Almirante Reis was still stylish. The district's image then took a nosedive but today, Intendente Square is the city's hotspot, evident from the guests to this hotel. Despite its black and white décor, the hotel still provides a feel-good factor. The excellent *Infâme* restaurant (see p.

★ **Home Lisbon Hostel**
Belongs to the world's best hostels, with "Mamma's Dinner"
→ p. 88

★ **Solar do Castelo**
Romantic hotel on the castle mound → p. 85

★ **Monte Belvedere**
Cool and casual → p. 86

★ **Palacio Ramalhete**
A stylish hideaway → p. 85

★ **Memmo Alfama**
Cosy despite all the designer furnishings. And a stunning terrace... → p. 84

MARCO POLO HIGHLIGHTS

60) is also used as the breakfast room and its high windows make you feel as if the outside is inside. *36 rooms | Largo do Intendente Pino Manique 6 | tel. 21 88 04 00 00 | www.1908lisboahotel. com | metro (green) Intendente*

CASA DE SÃO MAMEDE
(134 A3) (*K8*)

Quiet, small hotel in a pretty 18th-century town palace in the trendy Príncipe Real quarter. *28 rooms | Rua da Escola Politécnica 159 | tel. 213 96 31 66 | www.casadesaomamede.pt | metro (yellow) Rato*

INSPIRA SANTA MARTA
(134 C2) (*L7*)

Officially Portugal's greenest boutique hotel which supports the environment as well as social projects. Staff at this four-star accommodation are very helpful and the good restaurant offers gluten-free dishes. Beautiful Feng Shui rooms – little storage space and confusing light switches, but a central location in a delightful old-fashioned street parallel to the Avenida da Liberdade; you can reach the Rossio on foot in just 15 minutes. *89 rooms | Rua de Santa Marta 48 | tel. 210 44 09 00 | www.inspirahotels. com | metro (blue) Avenida | metro (blue, yellow) Marquês de Pombal*

MONTE BELVEDERE ★
(134 B5) (*L9*)

Cool boutique guesthouse in a beautiful old perfume factory from the 1930s. Clear lines, contemporary design, personal service – not forgetting its fabulous terrace with bar. The restaurant *Madame Petisca* is also open to non-hotel guests; large variety of unusual Portuguese tapas. **INSIDER TIP** Great for sundowner dinners. Reserve a table from 9 to 11 pm (rather than 7–9pm) and you'll be among locals. *9 suites | Rua Santa Catarina 17 | tel. 9 15 15*

MORE THAN A GOOD NIGHT'S SLEEP

Too cool for school!
Housed in the old palace, the *Hotel da Estrela* **(133 E1)** (*J–K8*) *(19 rooms | Rua Saraiva de Carvalho 35 | tel. 21 19 00 1 00 | www.hoteldaestrela.com | eléctrico 28 Rua Saraiva de Carvalho | metro (yellow) Rato | Moderate–Expensive)* was once a school and this theme continues in the hotel rooms with maps on the walls. There is a hospitality school next door. The hotel is located in the new trendy district of Campo de Ourique, the Estrela Park is around the corner and the city centre is close by. The restaurant's concept is unusual; the trainee chefs cook contemporary Portuguese cuisine and guests are invited to pay what they think is fair. Cool!

City trip with kids?
Yes, at the *Martinhal family hotel* **(120 A4)** (*M10*) *(37 studio apartments | from 200 euros | Rua das Flores 44 | tel. 210 02 96 00 | www.martinhal.com)*. Housed in a 19th-century Chiado palace, this hotel is designed with the needs of families in mind: furniture with no sharp edges, bunk beds (to add a sense of adventure!), bathrooms complete with baby tubs and potties. Babysitting services and organised activities for 0 to 9-year olds give parents time off... Information is provided in English on request. Breakfast (at an additional cost) is served next door at the *M Bar Family Café* (see p. 102).

Geared at global citizens – the Inspira Santa Marta Hotel and its restaurant

08 60 | www.shiadu.com | metro (blue, green) Baixa-Chiado

TESOURO DA BAIXA (120 C2) (𝄞 M9)

Although some complain that there are too many hotels in the Baixa, this brand-new boutique guesthouse is something special and already has a big following of fans. Spacious rooms with interesting views of the city. Pleasant design, contemporary and vintage touches, extremely friendly service and guest lounge with bar (guests are invited to write down what they drink – that's trust for you). The hotel couldn't be more centrally located if it tried. 33 rooms | Rua Dom Duarte 3 | tel. 9 14 17 69 69 | www.shiadu.com/tesouro-da-baixa | metro (green) Rossio | electrico 28 Martim Moniz

THE HOUSE (133 E3) (𝄞 J9)

Splendid boutique B&B in the quiet residential area of Estrela with a 🌿 360 de-grees panoramic terrace. Specially caters for visitors travelling alone. 9 rooms | Travessa Pinheiro 11 | 4th floor | tel. 2 15 94 79 49 | www.thehouse.pt | metro (yellow) Rato

TOREL PALACE (135 D3) (𝄞 M8)

Located on the tranquil Santana hill away from the crowds of tourists, this hotel is housed in a mansion from the turn of the century. The Baixa can be reached in a matter of minutes by taking the oldest funicular in Lisbon, as well as the hipster hotspot, Intendente, on the other side. With a pool. 26 rooms | Rua Câmara Pestana 23 | tel. 2 18 29 08 10 | www.torel palace.com | metro (blue) Restauradores, then Elevador do Lavra

ZUZA BED & BREAKFAST (120 B2) (𝄞 M9)

Couldn't be more central: elegant combination of B & B and apartments at Rossio.

The friendly owner has even designed his own city app for his guests! *4 rooms | Calçada do Duque 41 | tel. 9 34 44 55 00 | www.zuzabed.com | metro (blue, green) Baixa-Chiado*

HOTELS & GUESTHOUSES: BUDGET

ANJO AZUL (134 B–C4) (*M L9*)
Small, charming and gay-friendly pension in a quiet corner of the Bairro Alto. Offers very friendly service. All rooms with private bathroom, TV, DVD, Internet connection and mini bar. Ask for a 🌿 room on the third or fourth floor for more natural light and better views. *20 rooms |*

LOW BUDGET

Low-budget hotel booking: e.g. at *www.hostelbookers.com*

The *Lisbon Destination Hostel* **(120 B2)** (*M M9*) *(96 beds | from 22 euros/person, including breakfast| Largo do Duque de Cadaval 17 | tel. 2 13 46 64 57 | www.lisbon.destinationhostels.com | metro (green) Rossio)* is situated right on the second floor of the Neo-Moorish Rossio station and serves delicious food to its guests.

The ⭐ *Home Lisbon Hostel* **(121 D5)** (*M N9*) *(86 beds | from 12 euros/person | Rua S. Nicolau 13 | 2nd floor left | tel. 2 18 88 53 12 | www.homelisbonhotel.com | metro (blue, green) Baixa-Chiado)* was, in 2017, again named as the world's best medium-sized hostel. The owner's mother cooks for the guests.

Rua Luz Soriano 75 | tel. 2 13 47 80 69 and 2 13 46 71 86 | www.blueangelhotel.com | eléctrico 28 Calhariz (Bica)

HOTEL BOTÂNICO (134 B3) (*M L8*)
The rooms in this central and quiet three-star hotel are simple yet cosy, and the 🌿 upper floors have fine views across the city. Friendly service. *30 rooms | Rua Mãe d'Água 16–20 | tel. 2 13 42 03 92 | www.hotelbotanico.pt | metro (blue) Avenida*

LARGO RESIDENCIAS (135 D2–3) (*M N8*)
This cool, affordable artists' guesthouse is located 10 minutes from the centre on foot, right at the heart of the city's urban development scene, Largo do Intendente, with café bars, the hip Casa Independente and culture at your doorstep. If you want to go self-catering, the guesthouse has two kitchens and recreational room for all guests to use. The establishment is open to tourists as well as artists, looking to work on their projects in peace. *22 rooms | Largo do Intendente Pina Manique 19 | tel. 2 18 88 54 20 | www.largoresidencias.com | metro (green) Intendente*

PENSÃO LONDRES (134 C4) (*M L8–9*)
Guesthouse on the edge of the party quarter of Bairro Alto – hence the double-glazed windows. Rooms with and without a private bathroom; the ones that are en-suite also have air-conditioning. *36 rooms | Rua Dom Pedro V 53 | tel. 2 13 46 22 03 | www.pensaolondres.com.pt | bus 92 Rua Dom Pedro V*

PENSÃO PRAÇA DA FIGUEIRA (135 D4) (*M M9*)
Super-central, old-fashioned and well-run guesthouse on a square right next to Rossio. Some rooms have a private

bathroom; those that don't are very cheap indeed (30 euros). All rooms can receive the free WiFi signal. *34 rooms | Travessa Nova de São Domingos 9 | 3rd floor | tel. 213 42 43 23 | www.pensaopra cadafigueira.com | metro (green) Rossio*

RESIDENCIAL FLORESCENTE
(120 B1) (*M8*)
Comfortable but small rooms with WiFi, some with a balcony, and generous dorm-style rooms too. Restaurant with Portuguese cuisine which also offers a substantial breakfast. Extremely central location just a stone's throw from Rossio. *68 rooms | R. Portas de Santo Antão 99 | tel. 213 42 66 09 | www.residencialflores cente.com | metro (blue) Restauradores*

HOTEL ZENIT LISBOA (124 B5) (*L6*)
Four-star hotel belonging to a Spanish chain. Intimate, stylish and modern. Good value for money. *86 rooms | Av. 5 de Outubro 11 | tel. 213 10 22 00 | www.ze nithoteles.com | metro (yellow) Saldanha or Picoas*

APARTMENTS

The renting out of apartments has developed at a virtually explosive rate: especailly in the historical quarters, more and more Old Town houses are modernised and rented out to tourists. The top dog among the websites with apartment addresses is the controversial *airbnb.com* which acts as a "community" and has a rating system. Otherwise, you can also look at *www.citysiesta.com*. Another attractive district is the charming and historic worker's estate, *Vila Berta (www.mi casaenlisboa.com/apt/vila-berta)*.

CASA VILLA SERRA (120 C1) (*M8*)
The webiste offers apartments of varying sizes and styles in Pena, a central

yet untouristy part of town. Your host, a dynamic young American, will look after everything. Addresses are provided at booking. *Tel. 913 46 45 17 | www.visiting portugal.com/casavillaserra.htm | www. visiting portugal.com/santana.htm | metro (blue) Restauradores | metro (green) Rossio*

The key to happiness – from the bar straight to bed at Pensão Londres

CHIADO 16 (120 B5) (*M10*)
Four large, fancy B & B apartments sleeping 2–4 people in upmarket Chiado. Crystal chandeliers, breakfast brought to your room, high-speed internet – just cool! *Largo da Academia das Belas Artes 16 | tel. 213 94 16 16 | www. chiado-16.com | metro (green, blue) Baixa-Chiado*

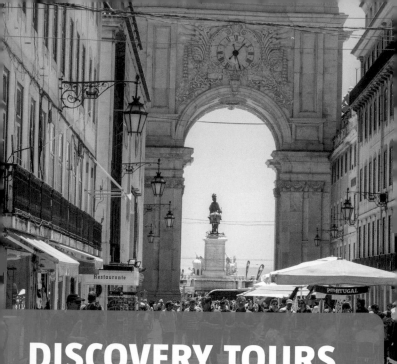

DISCOVERY TOURS

1 LISBON AT A GLANCE

START: ① Rossio
END: ⑯ Rua Nova do Carvalho

Distance:
➡ 6 km/3.7 mi

1 day
Walking time
(without stops)
1¾ hours

COSTS: 21.65 euros (1-day ticket for public transport 6.15 euros, ②
Triumphal arch 2.50 euros, ⑥ Castelo de São Jorge 8.50 euros, ⑪ Museu
Nacional de Arte Contemporânea do Chiado 4.50 euros) plus refreshments

IMPORTANT TIPS: Keep your wallets in a safe place when travelling on
the tram! Do not miss the free tour of ⑥ Castelo de São Jorge at 1pm!

Lisbon's appeal lies in its contrasting character which blends 3,000 years of history in the morbid charm of its crumbling facades with the vibrating pulse of a young and cosmopolitan city. This tour offers you a first glimpse at this city of light...

Would you like to explore the places that are unique to this city? Then the Discovery Tours are just the thing for you – they include terrific tips for stops worth making, breathtaking places to visit, selected restaurants and fun activities. It's even easier with the Touring App: download the tour with map and route to your smartphone using the QR Code on pages 2/3 or from the website address in the footer below – and you'll never get lost again even when you're offline.

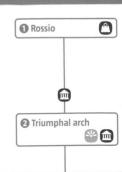

TOURING APP

→ p. 2/3

10:00am The tour starts at ❶ **Rossio** → p. 39. **Wander along the main boulevard Rua Augusta towards the River Tagus.** You are in the heart of the lower part of the city, the Baixa, lavishly constructed after the 1755 earthquake by the Marques of Pombal in its current grid pattern. The three-storey houses were constructed around the "Pombaline cage" structure: a symmetrical wood-lattice framework engineered to withstand earthquakes. You can climb up the imposing ❷ **Triumphal arch** *(admission 2.50 euros)* if you want to enjoy great views over Baixa, the Riv-

❶ Rossio

❷ Triumphal arch

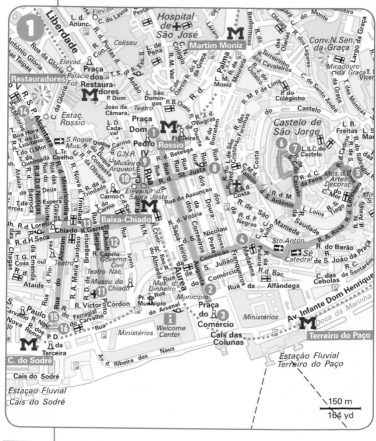

❸ Praça do Comércio ❗

❹ Eléctrico 28 🎫

er Tagus and **❸ Praça do Comércio** → p. 36. Then take a stroll across the city's square of commerce enclosed with yellow arcades.

11:30am Now head back towards Rossio and take a right into the **Rua Conceição**. Go down this street lined with old-fashioned shops selling colourful laces, buttons and crochet needles **until you reach the corner of Rua Madalena and its tram stop for the famous** tramway **❹ Eléctrico 28** → p. 26. Take this distinctive yellow tram, which has been running through the narrow streets of the old town for over 100 years, **a few stations further** – past the Cathedral Sé → p. 32 – until you reach **Largo das Portas do Sol**. From the scattering of terrace cafes, for example the ❺ **Esplanada das Portas do Sol → p. 32**, you'll get a splendid view over the rooftops of the Alfama and the Tagus. **Then climb up the steep, narrow set of steps Beco do Maldonado behind you and take a left into the crumbling yet picturesque Pátio de Dom Fradique –** a familiar setting if you have seen Wim Wenders' light-hearted film *Lisbon Story* (1994)...

`01:00pm` At this time of day, it's worth heading to ❻ **Castelo de São Jorge → p. 29** where the INSIDERTIP free English-language tour is about to begin. Despite the Moorish citadel being remodelled into a fairy-tale castle under Salazar's government, it still offers great views out over the city, a museum and an excavation site under its olive trees, pines and holm trees.

`02:00pm` Five minutes away on foot is the ❼ **Mercearia do Castelo** *(daily | Rua das Flores de Santa Cruz 2 | Moderate)* where you can enjoy lunch in the beautifully renovated Castelo quarter. **Once back in Baixa, go right along the Rua Cruz do Castelo, then right along the Rua do Milagro de Santo António** (with the white and blue painted tiles on the house facade) **to the Elevador da Baixa (entrance on the top deck of the Chão de Loureiro car park).** Take this elevator to the panoramic terrace of the INSIDERTIP ❽ **Cafeteria Pollux** *(Mon–Sat 10am–7pm | www.pollux.pt)* on the 9th floor. From this hardware store emporium, you have a direct view onto the Elevador de Santa Justa. **After a short break, take the Pollux elevator down to the 1st floor and head for the exit at Rua dos Fanqueiros.** You have now arrived at the ❾ **Elevador de Santa Justa → p. 35.** Avoid the long queue and **take the adjacent steps up to the Rua do Carmo and the elegant French-inspired district of Chiado → p. 39.** Directly opposite the steps leading upwards, you'll see the tiny shop ❿ **Luvaria Ulísses → p. 73** where you can buy elegant gloves in the finest leather at half the price you would otherwise pay back home. You may also catch the **Fadomobil** – a green vintage car selling CDs – which sometimes stops here where you can hear the legendary voice of Amália Rodrigues. **If not, head immediately up the Rua Garrett on your right and then left into the Rua Serpa Pinto.**

`04:00pm` The ⓫ **Museu Nacional de Arte Contemporânea do Chiado → p. 41** exhibits an excellent collection of contemporary Portuguese art. Cool retro souvenirs

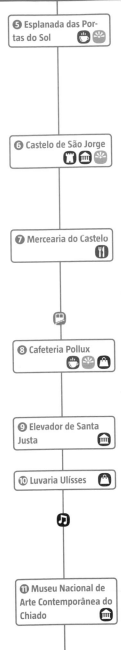

❺ Esplanada das Portas do Sol

❻ Castelo de São Jorge

❼ Mercearia do Castelo

❽ Cafeteria Pollux

❾ Elevador de Santa Justa

❿ Luvaria Ulísses

⓫ Museu Nacional de Arte Contemporânea do Chiado

⑫ A Vida Portuguesa

⑬ Café A Brasileira

⑭ 100 Maneiras

⑮ Pensão Amor

⑯ Rua Nova do Carvalho

are available from **⑫ A Vida Portuguesa → p. 70 in the parallel street Rua Anchieta.**

07:00pm For an aperitif close by, head to the legendary **⑬ Café A Brasileira → p. 59** where you can sit INSIDER TIP amongst locals in its wood-panelled interior instead of outside with the crowds of tourists and street musicians. *Jantar?* Supper? Starting with *bacalhau* served on a mini washing line, a tasting menu at **⑭ 100 Maneiras → p. 60** can take a while.

11:00pm Slowly the party really starts going! **Stroll down the typical Bairro street Rua do Diário das Notícias, right along the Rua do Norte, cross the Largo de Camoes and go down the Rua do Alecrim.** No. 19 offers a good stopover: The **⑮ Pensão Amor** *(closed Sun)* is a trendy bar with an interior design that reminds guests of its former life as a brothel. The hoards of night owls then head for the **⑯ Rua Nova do Carvalho**, painted in pink, the nightlife boulevard of Cais do Sodré → p. 74 – with Music Box Lisboa, Sol e Pesca and many more.

2 ARCHITECTURE AND "SEA BREEZE" – THE NEW LISBON

START: ❶ Gare do Oriente END: ❶ Gare do Oriente	¾ day Walking time (without stops) 1½ hours
Distance: 🚶 5.8 km/3.6 mi	

COSTS: 25.10 euros (1-day ticket for public transport 6.15 euros, ❻ Oceanário 15 euros, ❼ cable railway 3.95 euros) plus refreshments

IMPORTANT TIPS: Tickets for ❻ Oceanário are cheaper online! The Centro Comercial Vasco da Gama is open daily until midnight.

In its Parque das Nações, Lisbon has managed to achieve something which other cities unfortunately haven't: Originally built for the 1998 world expo, the site has become a well-integrated district in the city yet "saudade" → p. 24 is not to be felt here. On a stroll through the park, you'll rather encounter office workers and at the weekends joggers and young families.

11:00am Start at the iconic concrete structure of the **❶ Gare do Oriente**, where the red metro line stops. A

❶ Gare do Oriente

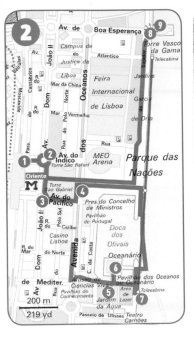

Shopper's paradise: the Vasco da Gama mall

central hub for national and international trains, this central station in white steel was originally designed by Santiago Calatrava for the Expo98 and resembles an airy forest of palm trees. **Take a left and cross the wide Avenida for a glimpse of the highly original ② Edifício Mythos** (2010) with its cleverly designed cladding structure and LEDs that create a multi-faceted and dynamic "fictional landscape". **To return, walk along the same side of the road past the Centro Comercial Vasco da Gama to another iconic piece of architecture:** the **③ Vodafone headquarters**, clearly visible in its trademark red and white corporate colours. Its curtain walling system alludes to the Casa dos Bicos → p. 29. On the river-facing side of the shopping centre, you'll be treated to the open-air, semi-abstract, monumental sculpture, the "**④ Sun Man**", by the Lisbon-born sculptor Jorge Vieira who died in the year of the expo. **Once you've reached the expo mascot** and the banks of the expansive River Tagus at this point, you can almost believe you've arrived at sea. **Go right and stroll around the wooden walkway circulating the water basin. On the opposite bank of the river, you'll be welcomed by**

② Edifício Mythos 🏢

③ Vodafone headquarters 🏢

④ Sun Man 🗿

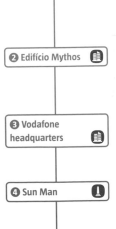

95

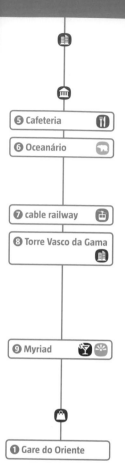

the **Portuguese Pavilion** designed by star architect Álvaro Siza Vieira with its roof made from reinforced concrete which bends like a sheet of paper. Take a peek into the – free! – exhibition of the Expo site *(Wed–Sat noon–6pm).* Nearby you can spot the gleaming-black **Casino Lisboa**.

01:00pm Enjoy lunch at the **5 Cafeteria** located on the first floor of the **Oceanarium** with its ceramic tile facade. The entrance is next to the ticket booths for the **6 Oceanário → p. 103**, where you can afterwards submerge into ocean life. The aquarium complex embodies the expo's theme "The Oceans, a Heritage for the Future".

05:00pm From the Oceanarium take the **7 cable railway** *(daily 11am–6 pm or 8pm | www.telecabinelisboa. pt)* to the foot of the **8 Torre Vasco da Gama,** Lisbon's highest building at 145 m (475 ft) high and a deliberate counterpart to the explorer's monument, the Padrão dos Descobrimentos → p. 48. Built to commemorate the 500th anniversary of Vasco de Gama's expedition to India, the tower's design resembles the prow of a caravel. You are not allowed up the tower so enjoy an aperitif instead on the terrace, *esplanada,* belonging to the Hotel **9 Myriad** built directly next to the tower. It is well worth paying that little bit extra: besides the free nibbles, you have the feeling to be literally sitting in the river below with a view onto the elegant **Vasco da Gama bridge. Now head along the River Tagus, through the Centro Comercial Vasco da Gama → p. 68 to the 1 Gare do Oriente. To experience the city by night, head back to the centre –** the expo site does not offer much in the way of nightlife...

| 5 Cafeteria |
| 6 Oceanário |
| 7 cable railway |
| 8 Torre Vasco da Gama |
| 9 Myriad |
| 1 Gare do Oriente |

3 A STROLL AROUND THE UPPER TOWN

START: **1** Praça dos Restauradores END: **15** Largo do Carmo	½ day Walking time (without stops) 45 minutes
Distance: ➡ 3 km/1.9 mi	
COSTS: 11.15 euros (1-day ticket for public transport 6.15 euros, **9** Convento dos Cardães 5 euros) plus refreshments	

The *miradouros* (literally "golden views") are amongst the most splendid sights Lisbon has to offer. This leisurely half-day stroll takes in splendid views, the more noble part of Bairro Alto, the trendy designer district of Príncipe Real and the city's hallmark cultural and shopping district of Chiado.

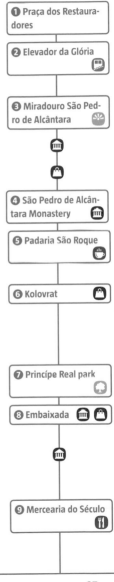

12:00pm The tour begins at **❶ Praça dos Restauradores** → p. 38. **A few steps further along the elegant boulevard Avenida da Liberdade, you'll come across the yellow funicular railway ❷ Elevador da Glória** → p. 34, **which will take you up into the upper town past the** INSIDER **TIP** street artist scene where graffiti artists are officially allowed to spray. **Next to the station at the top is the panoramic terrace ❸ Miradouro São Pedro de Alcântara** → **p. 41**, offering an amazing view onto the Castelo de São Jorge → p. 29. **Carry on uphill to the Rua Dom Pedro V., the more noble part of the Bairro Alto** district with its beautiful old city palaces, exclusive antique shops and designer stores. In the **❹ São Pedro de Alcântara Monastery** on the left, you can visit the INSIDER **TIP** church with its chapel adorned with beautiful marble inlays (free admission). A few steps further is the art nouveau bakery **❺ Padaria São Roque** (no. 57), also known as the *Catedral do Pão* (bread cathedral) – which offers WiFi! It's well worth seeing and ideal for a *Pastel-de-nata* break. One of the most interesting clothing shops on this designer stretch is **❻ Kolovrat** *(Mon–Sat 12.30–8pm | Rua Dom Pedro V 79 | www.lidjakolovrat.org)*. Croatian-born designer Lidja Kolovrat designs authentic and ecological clothing with leaf-style dresses and amusing handbags to be worn on the upper arm. You have now reached **Príncipe Real,** the city's designer district and home to the gay community.

02:00pm The secluded **❼ Príncipe Real park** is just a stone's throw away. On the other side of the road, you will not miss the former neo-Moorish aristocratic palace which is now the residence of **❽ Embaixada** *(www.embaixadalx. pt)* ("embassy"), a high-end shopping mall. At the **Ecolã Shop** you can get your hands on timeless classics such as jackets, handbags and accessories made of waterproof *burel* (loden cloth). **After taking a brief look around, head down the quieter Rua do Século past some splendid examples of 17th architecture and to the small, but nice ❾** INSIDER **TIP Mercearia do Século** *(Tue–Thu 9am–6pm, Fri/Sat 10am–11pm | Rua do Século 145 | Budget)* where friendly ladies serve unusual Portuguese snacks for lunch: tasty soups, bacalhau-bean stew, gluten-free desserts. Be-

❶ Praça dos Restauradores

❷ Elevador da Glória

❸ Miradouro São Pedro de Alcântara

❹ São Pedro de Alcântara Monastery

❺ Padaria São Roque

❻ Kolovrat

❼ Príncipe Real park

❽ Embaixada

❾ Mercearia do Século

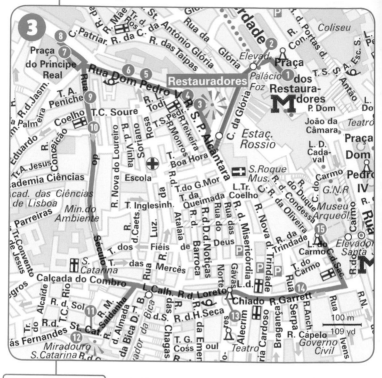

⑩ Convento dos Cardães

⑪ Miradouro de Santa Catarina

⑫ Noobai Café

hind number 123 hides the Carmelite Monastery **⑩ Convento dos Cardães** *(Mon–Sat 2.30–5.30 pm | www.conventodoscardaes.com)*, which not only survived the earthquake of 1755 but also the closing of the monasteries in 1834! **At the end of this road, take a left up the Calçada do Combro and then right onto the Rua Marechal Saldanha to the ⑪ Miradouro de Santa Catarina → p. 40.** Amongst the city's alternative reggae and guitar-playing community, you have a splendid view over the Tagus with the Ponte 25 de Abril → p. 53 and Cristo Rei Statue → p. 50 on the opposite bank. The **⑫ Noobai Café** *(daily 10am–midnight | www.noobaicafe.com)* resembles a bird's nest suspended on the Miradouro. Climb down through the roof to enter this café which is perfect for a *cafézinho* with a fantastic view.

04:00pm **Return to the Calçada do Combro and take a right past the** charming **Elevador da Bica** (the city's smallest elevator!) until you reach the square of the national poet ⑬ **Largo de Camões**, a popular meeting point for young people between Bairro Alto and Chiado. There is always plenty to see on the ⑭ **Rua Garrett** between the ancient façades of the noble jewellers, Europe's oldest book shop, **Livraria Bertrand** *(no. 73–75)*, and the colonial goods store **Casa Pereira** *(no. 38)*. **From this original cobbled street, take a left up the Calçada do Sacramento to the secluded** ⑮ **Largo do Carmo** with its monastery ruins **Igreja do Carmo** → p. 39 and cafés under Jacaranda trees. *Descanse um bocado!* – Give yourself some rest…

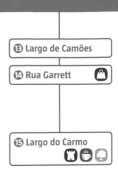

⑬ Largo de Camões

⑭ Rua Garrett

⑮ Largo do Carmo

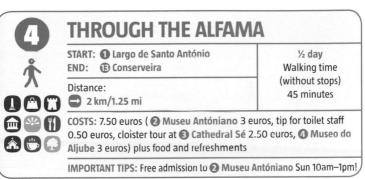

4 THROUGH THE ALFAMA

START: ① Largo de Santo António **END:** ⑬ Conserveira		½ day Walking time (without stops) 45 minutes
Distance: 🡆 2 km/1.25 mi		

COSTS: 7.50 euros (② **Museu Antóniano** 3 euros, tip for toilet staff 0.50 euros, cloister tour at ③ **Cathedral Sé** 2.50 euros, ④ **Museo do Aljube** 3 euros) plus food and refreshments

IMPORTANT TIPS: Free admission to ② **Museu Antóniano** Sun 10am–1pm!

Alfama is Lisbon's oldest district, a labyrinth of steep steps, narrow streets and quiet squares. For centuries, this Arabian quarter has been the shared home of workers, tradesmen and families from poorer backgrounds. Today this district is witnessing major renovation and artists' studios, boutiques and cool restaurants are popping up next to the district's traditional Fado bars and small corner shops.

10:30am The tour starts at ① **Largo de Santo António**. Lisbon's favourite saint is standing on this square: cast in bronze and with Jesus the Christ Child on his arm. The church of Saint Anthony of Lisbon is said to have been built on the site where this saint was born. The ② **Museu Antóniano** *(Tue–Sun 10am–6pm)* next door is also dedicated to this patron saint of lovers, of finding things and lost people! The city's INSIDER TIP cleanest and most charming public toilets are situated opposite the museum *(Mon–Sat 9.30am–1pm, 2–5.30pm)*… Up the hill, you'll notice Lisbon's oldest church, the formidable ③ **Cathedral Sé** → p. 32. **Follow the tram tracks and you'll reach the** ④ **Museo do Aljube** *(Tue–Sun 10am–6pm | admission 3 euros, free Sun 10am–1pm)* on your left-hand side, the

① Largo de Santo António

② Museu Antóniano

③ Cathedral Sé

④ Museo do Aljube

⑤ Fábula Urbis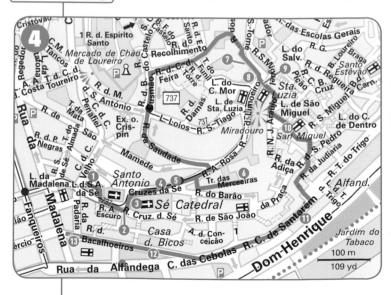

⑥ Memmo Alfama

⑦ Largo das Portas do Sol

⑧ garden café

former secret service prison under the Salazar dictatorship now open as a museum to the public. Booklovers will not be able to walk past the well-stocked bookshop **⑤ Fábula Urbis → p. 68**.

12:00pm The two-storey terrace of the trendy hotel **⑥ Memmo Alfama → p. 84** has now opened – slightly hidden from view, but with fabulous views and milky coffees. Just ask nicely at reception whether you are allowed on the *esplanada*. **Return to the Rua Augusto Rosa and take a left onto the Rua da Saudade past the ruins of the Roman city theatre** dating back to the time when Lisbon was still called Olisipo. From the 8th century, Alfama was used by the Arabic rulers as a Medina with the Castelo de Sao Jorge → p. 29 as a fortress. **Go right along the castle walls through the red gate of the noble residence Palácio Belmonte. Take a left heading downhill and then a right to ⑦ Largo das Portas do Sol**, where the official guardian saint of Lisbon, Sao Vicente, still guards over the city with a caravel under his arm.

01:00pm Fancy a bite to eat? An insider tip during the week is the **INSIDER TIP** affordable buffet served in the **⑧ garden café** of the pretty **Museu de Artes Decorativas → p. 33. Opposite the museum, head along the**

Casa dos Bicos: The façade of the city palais gave the "House of Spikes" its name

old Arabian city walls ⑨ **Cerca Moura and down the steps on the Rua Norberto Araújo to the mass of small streets below**. The houses are decorated with plant pots full of geranium blossoms, bird cages with chirping canaries, laundry and bunting blowing in the breeze. **Cross the Calçada da Figuera and the Beco da Corvinha down to** the richly adorned yet unfortunately seldom open **Church of** ⑩ **São Miguel**. On your right-hand side, you will be welcomed by one of the oldest houses in Alfama, painted in Bordeaux red with a projecting upper floor, wrestling for as much space as possible in this narrow street. **Go along the Rua de São Miguel to the right and take a left in front of** Torre de São Pedro de Alfama. The city's urban developments can be interpreted on the bare city walls. Hard to believe that an entire house once stood on this tiny cliff! **Proceed right past the old King's fountain** ⑪ **Chafariz d'El Rei**. At the Portuguese age of discovery, you had to queue at the six pumps according to status, gender and ethnic origin. The iconic piece of architecture ⑫ **Casa dos Bicos → p. 29** also originates from this period. **Rua dos Bacalhoeiros** is home to ⑬ **Conserveira** (no. 34) with its colourful cans of fish that make original and affordable souvenirs.

⑨ Cerca Moura

⑩ São Miguel

⑪ Chafariz d'El Rei

⑫ Casa dos Bicos

⑬ Conserveira

TRAVEL WITH KIDS

HIPPOTRIP (132 B5) (*[map] G11*)
Following a casual tour of the city in Portuguese and English, this yellow amphibian vehicle chugs down the Tagus River while onlookers grin and wave. Smaller children can get a booster seat. *Daily | 25 euros, children (allowed from 2 years) 15 euros | Doca de Santo Amaro | tel. 21 192 20 30 | www.hippotrip.com | eléctrico 15 Alcântara Mar*

JARDIM BORDALLO PINHEIRO
(138 C3) (*[map] O*)
The garden of the City Museum is filled with colourful animal sculptures inspired by legendary artist Rafael Bordalo Pinheiro (museum opposite). Monkeys hang in the trees, snails creep up walls. The (real) peacocks (an albino among them) don't know what to make of all this! *Tue–Sun 10am–1pm, 2–6pm | free admission | Campo Grande 245 | www.museudelisboa.pt | metro (yellow, green) Campo Grande*

JARDIM ZOOLÓGICO (138 C3) (*[map] O*)
Around 2,200 animals live in this zoo which is over 100 years old. And: a fairground, the feeding of the pelicans, a toy train and an aerial cableway. *Daily 10am–7pm, March–Sept until 8pm | admission 20.50 euros, children 3–11 years 14.50 euros | Estrada de Benfica 158–160 | www.zoo.pt | metro (blue) Jardim Zoológico*

INSIDER TIP ▶ LITTLE LISBON
This online platform is aimed at travellers with children and organises private family tours of the city. All the tours have a theme, for example the "Sea Heroes" tour or "Sintra for Young Explorers" and even food tours. The site also provides babysitting services and pushchair hire, etc. *Food tour 4 persons 220 euros, babysitting 8–20 euros/hr. | tel. 9 12 80 06 47 | www.lisbonforkids.com*

M BAR FAMILY CAFÉ (134 C5) (*[map] M10*)
Your young ones are made welcome in this bright, colourful and friendly family café in Chiado. The café serves food that your children enjoy and has a mini isetta car and other toys. *Daily 7.30am–7pm | Rua das Flores 44 | www.martinhal.com*

MUSEU DA CARRIS (132 B4) (*[map] G11*)
The tram museum has historic trams and buses, as well as conductor uniforms, timetables and photographs. An ancient tram takes visitors from one section to the next. *Mon–Sat 10am–6pm | admission 3 euros, children 1.50 euros (under*

Hard to choose between the sharks and a variety of other wild animals: do we go to the zoo or to the gigantic aquarium?

6 years free) | Rua Primeiro de Maio 101 | www.carris.pt | eléctrico 15 Santo Amaro

MUSEU DA MARIONETA
(134 A5) (*K10*)
Puppets, dolls and masks from all over the world in a restored monastery. *Tue–Sun 10am–1pm, 2–6pm | admission 5 euros, children up to 5 years 1.50 euros, up to 14 years 3 euros, Sun until 1pm free | Rua da Esperança 146 | www.museudamarioneta.pt | eléctrico 25 Santos-o-Velho*

OCEANÁRIO ● (123 F4) (*S3*)
The huge seawater aquarium houses around 15,000 marine-dwelling creatures. Particularly impressive is the main tank – a gigantic cylinder of glass. Sat at 9am there is INSIDER TIP aquarium music for children under 3, Sun *(1st and 2nd of the month 9am)* fado for children *(up to 4 years) (both: 35 euros (2 adults + child), admission fee and booking essential). Summer 10am–8pm, winter 10am–7pm | admission 15 euros, children 4–12 years*

10.80 euros, family ticket 39 euros | www.oceanario.pt | metro (red) Oriente

PARQUE DAS NAÇÕES
(123 E–F 1–4) (*S1–4*)
The Park of Nations has playgrounds, gardens, a "knowledge museum" for kids, a funicular and the Oceanarium *(see above)*. There is a skate park near the bridge. *Free admission, separate admission for the different sights | www.portaldasnacoes.pt | metro (red) Oriente*

PRAIA DE SANTO AMARO DE OEIRAS
(138 B4) (*0*)
Easy to reach (15 minutes from the Cais do Sodré) – Santo-Amaro beach offers everything for a fun family day out at the seaside: a child-friendly beach and rock pool for young nature explorers and a beach bar (as well as restaurants in the park behind the promenade). Nice for watching surfers outside the main summer season and: you can meet many Portuguese here...

FESTIVALS & EVENTS

Most banks and many, though not all, shops are closed on public holidays. December 26th and Easter Monday are normal workdays. Museums are usually closed on Jan 1st, Easter Sunday, May 1st and December 25th.

The city on the Tagus loves to party, and there are plenty of occasions for Lisboetas to celebrate something or other all year round (info at *www.visitlisboa.com* and *www.viralagenda.com*). The biggest party month is June, when Lisbon's many popular saints are honoured, especially Santo António on the 13th.

FESTIVALS & EVENTS

MARCH

Middle of the month: *Moda Lisboa/ Fashion Week (Pavilião Carlos Lopes/ Parque Eduardo VII | www.modalisboa. pt)*. Also in Oct.

APRIL

25 April: *Parade* of the Communist Party (PCP) along Avenida da Liberdade
Late April: *Dias da música (www.ccb.pt)*, three-day classical music marathon at the Centro Cultural de Belém; late April (10 days): *Indie Lisboa (indielisboa.com)*, international festival of independent film

MAY

Sun following 4 May: *Procissão de Nossa Senhora de Saúde*, procession of Our Dear Lady of Health through Mouraria, commemorating the end of the plague epidemic of 1580, oldest procession in town!
Early May: *Feira do Livro (afternoons, Fri–Sun until 11pm | www.feiradolivrode lisboa.pt | metro (blue, yellow) Marquês de Pombal)*; book fair in the Parque Eduardo VII

JUNE/JULY

For nearly the entire month, the so-called *Arraials* are celebrated: street parties with music and dance, grilled sardines and a lot of wine.
A highlight is on 12 June, the night before the Dia de Santo António: *Casamentos de Santo António*, couples from disadvantaged backgrounds can have their nuptials sponsored by the city. In the Sé and the Câmara Municipal (city hall) from 2pm
For a hip neighbourhood INSIDER TIP *Arraial (www.renovaramouraria.pt)* with less of a scrum, check out the one in Mouraria. One of the highlights: the *Marchas populares* parade *(from 9pm | Avenida da Liberdade)*

Jazz, pop and classical music festivals – but Lisbon's saints give rise to the biggest parties. Long live Santo António & Co.!

Lisboa em festa (www.egeac.pt | www.cm-lisboa.pt), exhibitions, markets and concerts

Early July: **NOS Alive** (www.nosalive.com), three days with big names in pop and rock in Algés on the western fringes of the city

Early July: **Sintra Festival** (www.cm-sintra.pt), two-weeks of classical music and dance in Sintra and Queluz

Mid-July: **Superbock Superrock** (www.superbocksuperrock.pt), rock festival in the Parque das Nações

July: **Festival Cool Jazz** (www.edpcooljazz.com), open-air jazz concerts

AUGUST

Early Aug: **Jazz em Agosto** (www.musica.gulbenkian.pt/jazz), international, high-calibre jazz festival (10 days)

DECEMBER

Pre-Christmas concerts in many churches, mostly free! www.egeac.pt

NATIONAL HOLIDAYS

1 Jan	New Year's Day
25 Feb 20, 16 Feb 21, 1 March 22	
	Carnaval/Entrudo (Shrove Tuesday)
10 April 20, 2 April 21, 15 April 22	
	Sexta-feira Santa (Good Friday)
12 April 20, 4 April 21, 17 April 22	
	Páscoa (Easter Sunday)
25 April	*Dia da Liberdade*
1 May	Labour Day
11 Jun 20, 3 Jun 21, 16 June 22	
	Corpus Christi
10 June	*Dia de Portugal/ Dia de Camões*
15 Aug	Assumption
5 Oct	Day of the Republic
1 Nov	All Saints
1 Dec	*Dia da Restauração*
8 Dec	Immaculate Conception
25 Dec	Christmas

LINKS, BLOGS, APPS & MORE

LINKS & BLOGS

www.lisbontrail.com The graffiti scene is a major part of Lisbon's culture. This English-language website previews highlights such as the monster creations by Brazilian graffiti artists Os Gemeos (The Twins) on the Avenida Fontes Pereira de Melo

www.babbel.com Portuguese online language course (no software download required), with free training app

www.lx3d.com Impressive three-dimensional photographs of Lisbon

www.camillawatsonphotography. net Website with photo gallery by an English photographer who focuses on social themes in her work such as a portrait gallery in tribute of her neighbours printed on the walls around her studio, a photographic **INSIDER TIP** *fado route* along the atmospheric Rua do Capelão and pinhole photography courses for children. All projects are intended to revitalise the old Moorish quarter of Mouraria

www.couchsurfing.org Lisbon's friendly couch surfing community is very active with many sub-communities organising activities, language learning exchange etc. You can also contact the co-author of this book (Username: KATHLEENLX)

www.golisbon.com/blog Continually updated and always interesting blog on nightlife, gastro scene, etc. by a lisboeta originally from New York

www.expat.com/en/network/europe/portugal/lisbon If you're planning to spend a little longer in the city, you may like to share your experiences with other expats. You can find them on this online platform

www.inlovewithlisbon.com Wide-ranging blog by a Lisbon lover – including recipes, poems and a long list of more blogs

Regardless of whether you are still researching your trip or already in Lisbon: these addresses will provide you with more information, videos and networks to make your holiday even more enjoyable

www.meetup.com New people meet up and learn something new on this site: The meet-up phenomenon from the USA has now gripped Lisbon. Yoga lovers, nature enthusiasts, geeks – there is something here for virtually everyone. Meetings are free or you just pay a small contribution

www.newmediarepublic.com/azulejos A lively and passionate history of Lisbon's azulejos, in English

VIDEOS & MUSIC

vimeo.com/103266746 This is Lisbon: A Ukraine-born local has produced a homage to this city, in a time-lapse video with a touch of Sesimbra beach flair and Morcheeba sound track in the background

www.youtube.com/watch?v=3B8JAuRHftU The modern-folk veterans Dead Combo in the insider cultural spot Casa Independente – homage to the multicultural hip side of Lisbon: "Lisboa Mulata"

vimeo.com/182015533 Caught between its past and future: an exciting case study on the effects of tourism and gentrification in the old Moorish neighbourhood, Mouraria

APPS

Lisbon Guide Good-value iPhone-App by the tried-and-tested *Spotted By Locals community (www.spottedbylocals.com):* Lisboners old and new enthusiastically share the gems they find – restaurants, markets, parks, shops, etc.

ShakeItPhoto app Lisbon is the city of nostalgia and with the ShakeItPhoto mobile app from Banana Camera you can take iPhone photos in good old Polaroid style, so-called "fauxlaroids". For 1.99 euros at iTunes; for Android users, instant is available for 1.88 euros

INSIDER TIP *Mygon* The coupon app *(www.mygon.com)* allows you to browse all the deals and last minute discounts that are taking place near you. It is also available on the Mygon website: simply reserve a table at a local restaurant for free using Mygon, notify the restaurant that you're coming via Mygon and then pay

TRAVEL TIPS

ARRIVAL

🚗 Driving to Lisbon is really only recommended if Lisbon is a stop-over on a longer trip. Less tiring, if much more expensive, are car trains. The green insurance card is obligatory. Driving around the city can be pretty stressful: there is little street parking and traffic is heavy. Taxis are cheap here, and the urban transport system will take you to most places.

🚆 Taking the train from London to Paris (*www.cp.pt*, *www.seat61.com*), and from there to Hendaye/Irun and on by Sul-Express to Lisbon for an early-morning arrival, has its charm and is the eco option, but it is costly (approx. 400 euros) and time-consuming (about 24 hrs.). Those who are able to combine visiting Lisbon with other European stops are well served by an InterRail ticket.

🚌 Eurolines serves Lisbon from London. The journey takes around 36 hours and costs around 100 pounds. *www. eurolines.co.uk*

✈ Many airlines serve Lisbon on non-stop services. With a bit of luck, you'll find a flight for as little as 80 pounds (*easyJet, bmibaby, Thomson*). Flight time is approx. 2.5 hrs. Flights from Boston (*SATA*) or New York (*United, TAP*) cost from 600 dollars upwards and take 6.5 hrs. Humberto Delgado airport is approx. 10 km (6 miles) north of the city centre. Metro link to Rossio for example: take the red line to Alameda then change to the green line (*1.50 euros, plus 50 cents for a multi-journey ticket, see Public Transport*). The shuttlebus into the city starts outside Arrivals (*8am–11pm every 20 minutes | 3.50 euros | www.aerobus.pt*); large suitcases will only be admitted on this bus. A taxi into the city centre costs around 12 euros, meaning the taxi vouchers for sale at the tourist info in the arrivals hall for 21 euros are not exactly a good deal. However, there are rip-off taxi drivers, so you're best off heading for the taxi rank outside Departures (*Partidas*).

RESPONSIBLE TRAVEL

It doesn't take a lot to be environmentally friendly whilst travelling. Don't just think about your carbon footprint whilst flying to and from your holiday destination but also about how you can protect nature and culture abroad. As a tourist it is especially important to respect nature, look out for local products, cycle instead of driving, save water and much more. If you would like to find out more about eco-tourism please visit: *www.ecotourism.org*

BANKS & CREDIT CARDS

Opening times: Mon–Fri 8.30am–3pm. Use your direct debit or credit card to draw money from cashpoints (*Multibanco*). Foreign credit cards are usually only accepted in major stores, restaurants, hotels, etc. Small shops and taxi drivers sometimes have difficulties providing change even for 20-euro notes.

CAR HIRE

All the major providers (*Hertz, Avis*, etc.) are present in Lisbon; one money-saving choice is *InterRent* at the airport and inside the Santa Apolónia train station *(www2.interrent.com)*. A national driving licence is sufficient, but be aware of not just the obligatory seat belt, but also the obligation to carry a fluorescent vest. Penalties for offences are high! Speed limits: on country roads 90km/h (55mph), on motorways 120km/h (75mph), for those who have had their permit for less than a year 90km/h (55mph). Drink-driving limit: 0.5. 24-hour breakdown service: ACP *(Automóvel Clube de Portugal)* | *tel. 8 08 22 22 22* | *www.acp.pt)*. A scooter can be hired at *Lx Rent a Scooter (daily 9.30am–6.30pm | Campo das Cebolas 21 | www.lxrentascooter.pt)*.

CITY TOURS

BIKEIBERIA
Friendly bike tours through the city, also bike hire. Very popular: INSIDER TIP Cycle to Belém, take the Trafaria ferry – there's no faster way to São-João beach on the Costa da Caparica. *Largo Corpo Santo 5 | tel. 2 13 47 03 47 | 9 69 63 03 69 | www.bikeiberia.com*

HALCYON
INSIDER TIP sailing trips are launched on the beautifully restored "Halcyon": exclusive trips taking in the Docas and the foot of the Alfama for small groups of 2 people and more. New: trips now take place daily, speak to skipper Luis! Or how about a New Year's Eve trip with fireworks? *Booking required | from 45 euros | Doca de Alcântara | pier 701 | tel. 9 13 67 19 56 | eléctrico 15 Cais da Rocha | bus 714 Praça da Armada, look out for wooden pavilion of Cafetaria Nacional*

LISBOA AUTÊNTICA
Highly original city tours organised by a young and enthusiastic team, e.g. "Lisbon Essential" with practical tips *(3 hrs., from 3 people, pre-booking required, 35 euros including drink, dessert and public transport)*. Or ride up the picturesque, albeit steep Serra de Sintra – a breeze on an electric bike! INSIDER TIP Culinary tours available from 40 euros a person for groups of two persons and more. *Tel. 9 13 22 17 90 | 9 69 23 38 91 | www.lisboaautentica.com*

CURRENCY CONVERTER

£	€	€	£
1	1.15	1	0.87
3	3.45	3	2.61
5	5.74	5	4.35
13	14.93	13	11.32
40	46	40	35
75	86	75	65
120	138	120	104
250	287	250	218
500	574	500	435

$	€	€	$
1	0.88	1	1.13
3	2.64	3	3.40
5	4.41	5	5.67
13	11.46	13	14.75
40	35	40	45
75	66	75	85
120	106	120	136
250	220	250	284
500	441	500	567

For current exchange rates see www.xe.com

LISBON BY BOAT ●

Learn more about the city on these pleasant river tours where guests are served cheese from Azores accompanied by beer, coffee or tea. The sails are hoisted when the wind gets up. It's worth combining a river tour with a day in Belém: The bus stop with ticket sales and the marina jetty (Doca de Belém) are located on the left when you come up from the subway, approaching from the Hieronymus Monastery. *www.lisbonbyboat.com*

MOURARIA GUIDED TOURS

Guided tours in two languages (Portuguese, English) through this quarter which blends tradition with trend. Meeting point: church of Nossa Senhora da Saúde (135 D4) (*Ø N8*) *Sat 3pm | Martim Moniz | Facebook | eléctrico 28 | metro (green) Martim Moniz*

TUK-TUK

Originating from Asia, these colourful little vehicles can be seen flying through the narrow streets everywhere in the city and are parked waiting for passengers in front of the cathedral, along the Rua de Julião in Baixa or the Rua Garret in Chiado. Take one of the electric, silent models, for example from ⊙ *Ecotuktours*. *www.ecotuktours.com*

WILD WALKERS ● (120 A4) (*Ø M9*)

Rather than "wild", these city tours are original and lively. Mon, Wed, Fri they explore modern Lisbon; Thu, Sat, Sun the old town. Everything is organised on a tip-basis *(recommended amount: 4–5 euros). Daily 10.30 am | meeting point at Rossio, at the fountain in front of the statue (look out for a red t-shirt) | www.wildwalkers.eu | metro (green) Rossio.* The "wild walkers" also organise fado evenings on Wed, Sat and Sun *(meeting point at Rossio, 8.30 pm)* (fixed price including drinks 30 euros, 25 euros for Walk participants). A pub crawl through Bairro Alto is also held at 11 pm organised by a Portuguese party team. A young crowd offering a first, affordable glimpse of Lisbon in the evening *(meeting point Largo Luis de Camões | in summer daily, in winter Mon, Wed–Sat | 15 euros incl. generous drinks | metro (blue, green) Baixa-Chiado).*

CONSULATES & EMBASSIES

UK EMBASSY

Rua de São Bernardo 33 | 1249-082 Lisboa | tel. 351 21 392 40 00 | ukinportugal.fco.gov.uk/en/

US EMBASSY

Avenida das Forças Armadas | 1600-081 Lisboa | tel. 351 21 727 3300 | https://pt.usembassy.gov/

CUSTOMS

Within the EU, tourists may freely import and export goods for personal use, incl. as a guideline: 800 cigarettes, 10 litres spirits and 90 litres wine. North American citizens are subject to much lower allowances, and be aware that carrying personal defence sprays and other arms is illegal in Portugal.

EMERGENCY

Police, accidents: *tel. 112* (national)

HEALTH

The EHIC European health insurance card is valid in Portugal. Embassies and airlines have lists of English-speaking doctors, though most Portuguese medical staff will speak English. Accident & Emergency: *Hospital de São José (Rua*

José António Serrano | tel. 218 84 10 00 | metro: Martim Moniz)

INFORMATION IN ADVANCE

PORTUGUESE NATIONAL TOURIST OFFICE
11, Belgrave Square | London, SW1X 8PP | tel. 020 72 01 66 66 | www.visitportugal.com

PORTUGUESE NATIONAL TOURIST OFFICE
866 Second Avenue, 8th Floor | New York, NY 10017 | www.visitportugal.com

TURISMO DE LISBOA
Rua do Arsenal, 23 | tel. 210 31 27 00 | www.visitlisboa.com

INFORMATION IN LISBON

TOURIST INFORMATION (TURISMOS)
– Palácio Foz | Praça dos Restauradores | tel. 213 64 33 14 | www.askmelisboa.com | daily 9am–8pm | metro (blue) Restauradores
– Humberto Delgado Airport (Arrivals) | tel. 218 45 06 60 | daily 7am–midnight
–Santa Apolónia Station | Terminal Internacional | tel. 218 82 16 06 | Mon–Sat 8am–1pm
– Lisboa Welcome Center | Praça do Comércio | tel. 210 31 28 10 | daily 9am–8pm | metro (blue) Terreiro do Paço

PERSONAL SAFETY

Compared to other European countries, the crime rate in Portugal remains low, but pick-pocketing has risen considerably. The major tourist attractions attract pick-pockets, particularly in the tram No. 28 or the Baixa pedestrian zone. Keep your valuables in the hotel safe and carry only the amount of cash you really need.

PHONE & MOBILE PHONE

Although EU mobile roaming charges have been dropped, this does not mean that the same flat rate applies to the UK network as it does to the Portuguese network. The conditions of your contract and mobile operator apply for mobile surfing. **INSIDER TIP** You can charge your mobile with a power bank in the 7th floor coffee shop at the Corte Inglés department store (20 euros deposit | Mon–Sat 10am–9pm, Sun 10am–8pm).

Tel. dialling code for Portugal: 00351; for UK from Portugal: 0044; for Ireland 00353; for USA: 001.

POLICE

The police station serving tourists (PSP-Esquadra de Turismo) stays open 24 hours, and English is spoken. Tel.

BUDGETING

Wine	£10.25/$13.50
	for a bottle of house wine
Public transport	£5.25/$7
	for a one-day travelcard
Espresso	£0.50/$0.68
	for a cup
Cake	£0.85–3.40/$1.15–4.50
	for a piece
CD	£10.25/$13.60
	CD of Portuguese music
Fado	£17/$22.50
	minimum consumption in a major fado venue

213 42 16 23 | Palácio Foz | next to the Turismo on Praça dos Restauradores | metro (blue) Restauradores

POST

Opening times of the post offices: Mon–Fri 9am–6pm. Main post office at Praça dos Restauradores: Mon–Fri 8am–10pm,

Sat/Sun 9am–6pm. Stamps *(selos)* can also be bought at machines and in hotels. Letters are *cartas*, postcards *postais*. Postage for letters as well as cards within Europe is 80 cents. Be careful: Some souvenir shops will try to sell them for 1 euro, the value is not shown on the stamp! Letterboxes are red, Express mail *(Correio Azul)* (more expensive) blue. A postcard to Britain will take around 3–5 days, slightly longer for North America.

PUBLIC TRANSPORT

Carris runs the city buses, *eléctricos* (trams, recognised by the E behind the line number) and elevadores (lifts). Network maps are displayed at bus stops or can be downloaded at *www.carris.pt*. Running between 6.30am and 1am, the Metro (*www.metrolisboa.pt*) is fast and comfortable. A journey within the city centre costs 1.50 euros. The easiest and cheapest way is to use rechargeable chip cards which are valid for all types of public transport and on which you can load money. The white or green *7-colinas* or *viva-viagem* ticket costs 0.50 euros, for *zapping* (recharging) from 5 euros. You can buy them at Metro stations, in the Casa da Sorte, Praça da Figueira and post offices and you can transfer money onto the cards here too. A 1-day ticket for metros, trams (including the 28E), buses, funiculars and elevadores costs 6.15 euros. The machines at the Metro stations have instructions in English; it's best to have small change on you.

The *Turismos* promote and sell the *Lisboa Card*, which includes use of all public transport and free or discounted entry

WEATHER IN LISBON

	Jan	Feb	March	April	May	June	July	Aug	Sept	Oct	Nov	Dec
Daytime temperatures in °C/°F	14/57	15/59	17/63	20/68	21/70	25/77	27/81	28/82	26/79	22/72	17/63	15/59
Nighttime temperatures in °C/°F	8/46	8/46	10/50	12/54	13/55	15/59	17/63	17/63	17/63	14/57	11/52	9/48
Sunshine hours/day	5	6	6	9	10	11	12	11	9	8	6	5
Precipitation days/month	11	8	11	7	7	2	1	1	4	7	9	11
Water temperature in °C/°F	14/57	14/57	14/57	15/59	16/61	17/63	18/64	19/66	19/66	18/64	16/61	15/59

to museums and sights. The *Lisboa Card* costs 18.50 euros for 24 hours, 31.50 euros for 48, and 39 for 72 hrs. Have a good think about your itinerary though: the card is only really worth getting if you plan to visit a lot of museums (also remember than many museums offer free admission on Sunday mornings and most are closed on Mondays) and want to go to Sintra, too. Info: *www.askmelisboa.com*.

Passenger ferries run every 20 minutes from about 5.30am to 2am. Ferry terminals: Cais do Sodré, Terreiro do Paço and Belém. Ticket prices for a trip across the Tagus range between 1.15 and 2.70 euros. *www.transtejo.pt*.

Suburban trains *(Comboio suburbano)*: trains to Estoril/Cascais leave every 20 minutes from Cais do Sodré. Ticket 2.20 euros. The journey to Cascais (via other stops with beach facilities, including Carcavelos) lasts approx. 35 minutes. Trains to Sintra depart every 20 min. from Rossio train station, journey time 45 min., ticket 4.60 euros return, *www.cp.pt*. **INSIDER TIP** It's definitely worth buying the zapping card beforehand to avoid the long queues! There are different combination tickets available to ride with the train/bus and visit palaces such as the Sintra Green Card. One alternative is the new 10.15 euro ticket valid for 24 hours on all means of transport within Lisbon as well as in Sintra and Cascais.

Buses run by *TST (www.tsuldo tejo.pt)* run to Costa da Caparica, the starting point for miles and miles of beaches; departures from Praça Espanha (no. 153) and Areeiro (No. 161). The return journey costs about 7.50 euros. Carris beach shuttle in the main season.

TAXI

Taxis in Lisbon are cheap. Lisbon's taxis are mostly black with a green roof. Call a taxi: *Radio Taxis de Lisboa | tel. 2 18 11 11 11*. The meter is set to 3.90 euros at the start, luggage (1.60 euros) and taxi call (0.80 euros) cost extra. Occasionally, there are rip-off taxi drivers waiting at the airport; only pay the amount which is on the taximeter and, if in doubt, ask to be driven to the next *esquadra* (police station). Despite hostility from taxi drivers and lobbyists, the credit card-based *Uber app* for smartphones is now legal in Lisbon. *Cabify* is also present.

TIME

Portugal runs on Greenwich time, i.e. British and Irish visitors don't need to set their watches.

TICKET SALES

Tickets for arts and sports events are available from the following sales points: *ABEP Kiosk (Praça dos Restauradores | Av. da Liberdade | near main post office and Turismo | metro (blue) Restauradores); Fnac (Armazéns do Chiado | daily 10am–11pm | www.fnac.pt | metro (blue, green) Baixa-Chiado)*

TIPPING

A *gorjeta* is always appreciated for service. At restaurants, this ranges between 5 and 10% of the amount; at lunchtime or in a café, less is okay, too.

WIFI

Free WiFi is spreading across the city; with an online connection, you have access to all information about what's happening in the city. For WiFi-free zones, Vodafone *(www.vodafone.pt)* offers a package with 5GB data plus national and international text messages for 20 euros.

USEFUL PHRASES PORTUGUESE

PRONUNCIATION

To help you say the Portuguese words we have added a simple pronunciation guide in square brackets and an apostrophe ' before the syllable that is stressed. Note the following sounds shown in the pronunciation guide:
"zh" like the "s" in "pleasure", "ng" indicates a nasal sound at the end of a word (i.e. not with distinct consonants as in English) , e.g. "não" is shown as "nowng", "ee" as in "fee", "ai" as in "aisle", "oo" as in "zoo"

IN BRIEF

Yes/No/Maybe	sim [seeng]/não [nowng]/talvez [tal'vesh]
Please	se faz favor [se fash fa'vor]
Thank you	obrigado (m)/obrigada (f) [obri'gadoo/obri'gada]
Sorry/ Excuse me, please	Desculpa! [dish'kulpa]/Desculpe! [dish'kulp]
May I...?/ Pardon?	Posso...? ['possoo]/ Como? ['komoo]
I would like to...	Queria... [ke'ria]
Have you got...?	Tem...? [teng]
How much is...	Quanto custa...? ['kwantoo 'kooshta]
good/bad/broken/ doesn't work	bem [beng]/mal [mal]/estragado [ishtra'gadoo]/ não funciona [nowng fung'siona]
too much/much/little	demais [de'maish]/muito ['mooitoo]/pouco ['pokoo]
all/nothing	tudo ['toodoo]/nada ['nada]
Help!/Attention!/Caution!	Socorro! [soo'korroo]/Atenção! [atten'sowng]
ambulance	ambulância [amboo'langsia]
police/fire brigade	polícia [pu'lisia]/bombeiros [bom'beyroosh]
prohibition/forbidden	interdição [interdi'sowng]/proibido [prooi'bidoo]
danger/dangerous	perigo [pe'rigoo]/perigoso [peri'gosoo]

GREETINGS, FAREWELL

Good morning!/after-noon!/evening!/night!	Bom dia! [bong 'dia]/Bom dia! [bong 'dia]/ Boa tarde! ['boa 'tard]/Boa noite! ['boa 'noyt]
Hello!/Goodbye!	Olá! [o'la]/Adeus! [a'dy-oosh]
See you	Ciāo! [chowng]
My name is...	Chamo-me... ['shamoo-me]
What's your name?	Como se chama? ['komoo se 'shama] Como te chamas? ['komoo te 'shamas]
I'm from...	Sou de... [so de]

Falas português?

"Do you speak Portuguese?" This guide will help you to say the basic words and phrases in Portuguese

DATE & TIME

Monday/Tuesday	segunda-feira [se'goonda 'feyra]/terça-feira ['tersa 'feyra]
Wednesday/Thursday	quarta-feira ['kwarta 'feyra]/quinta-feira ['kinta 'feyra]
Friday/Saturday	sexta-feira ['seshta 'feyra]/sábado ['sabadoo]
Sunday	domingo [doo'mingoo]
today/tomorrow/ yesterday	hoje ['ozhe]/amanhã [amman'ya]/ ontem ['onteng]
hour/minute	hora ['ora]/minuto [mi'nootoo]
day/night/week	dia [dia]/noite [noyt]/semana [se'mana]
month/year	mês [meysh]/ano ['anoo]
What time is it?	Que horas são? [ke 'orash sowng]
It's three o'clock	São três horas. [sowng tresh 'orash]
It's half past three	São três e meia. [sowng tresh i 'meya]

TRAVEL

open/closed	aberto [a'bertoo]/fechado [fe'shadoo]
entrance	entrada [en'trada]
exit	saída [sa'ida]
departure/arrival	partida [par'tida]/chegada [she'gada]
toilets/restrooms/ ladies/gentlemen	sanitários [sanni'tariush]/ senhoras [sen'yorash]/ senhores [sen'joresh]
(no) drinking water	água (não) potável ['agwa (nowng) po'tavel]
Where is...?/Where are...?	Onde é...? ['onde e]/Onde são...? ['onde sowng]
left/right	à esquerda [a ish'kerda]/à direita [a dee'reyta]
straight ahead/back	em frente [eng 'frente]/para atrás ['para'trash]
bus	autocarro [auto'karroo]
stop	paragem [pa'razheng]
parking lot	estacionamento [eshtassiona'mentoo]
street map/map	mapa ['mappa]/mapa da cidade ['mappa da see'dad]
train station/ harbour/ airport	estação ferroviária [eshta'sowng ferrovi'aria]/ porto ['portoo]/aeroporto [a-eyro'portoo]
schedule/ticket	horário [o'rariyu]/bilhete [bil'yet]
single/return	só ida [so 'ida]/ida e volta ['ida i 'vollta]
train/platform	comboio [kom'boyoo]/linha ['linya]
I would like to rent...	Gostaria de alugar... [goshta'ria de alloo'gar]
a car/a bicycle/ a boat	um carro [oong 'karroo]/uma bicicleta [ooma bissi'kletta]/um barco [oong 'barkoo]
petrol/gas station/ petrol/gas / diesel	bomba de gasolina ['bomba de gaso'lina]/ petróleo [pe'troleo]/gasóleo [ga'soleo]
breakdown/repair shop	avaria [ava'ria]/garagem [ga'razheng]

FOOD & DRINK

Could you please book a table for tonight for four?	Se faz favor, pode reservar-nos para hoje à noite uma mesa para quatro pessoas. [se fash fa'vor, 'pode reser'varnoosh 'para 'oshe ah noit ooma 'mesa 'para 'kwatroo pe'ssoash]
The menu, please	A ementa, se faz favor. [a i'menta, se fash fa'vor]
bottle/glass	garrafa [gar'raffa]/copo ['koppoo]
salt/pepper/sugar	sal [sall]/pimenta [pi'menta]/açúcar [a'ssookar]
vinegar/oil	vinagre [vi'nagre]/azeite [a'zeite]
milk/cream/lemon	leite ['leyte]/natas ['natash]/limão [li'mowng]
with/without ice/sparkling	com [kong]/sem [seng] gelo ['zheloo]/gás [gash]
vegetarian/allergy	vegetariano/-a [vezhetari'anoo/-a]/alergia [aller'zhia]
May I have the bill, please?	A conta, se faz favor. [a 'konta, se fash fa'vor]

SHOPPING

Where can I find...?	Quero... ['keroo]/Procuro... [pro'kooroo]
pharmacy/chemist	farmácia [far'massia]/drogaria [droga'ria]
baker/market	padaria [pada'ria]/mercado [mer'kadoo]
shopping centre	centro comercial ['sentroo kommer'ssial]
100 grammes/1 kilo	cem gramas [seng 'grammash]/um quilo [oong 'kiloo]
expensive/cheap/price	caro ['karoo]/barato [ba'ratoo]/preço ['pressoo]
more/less	mais [maish]/menos ['menoosh]

ACCOMMODATION

I have booked a room	Reservei um quarto. [rezer'vey oong 'kwartoo]
Do you have any... left?	Ainda tem...? [a'inda teng]
single room	um quarto individual [oong 'kwartoo individu'al]
double room	um quarto de casal [oong 'kwartoo de ka'sal]
breakfast/ half board/ full board (American plan)	pequeno-almoço [pe'kaynoo al'mossoo]/ meia pensão ['meya pen'sowng]/ pensão completa [pen'sowng kom'pleta]
shower/sit-down bath	ducha [doosha]/banho ['banyoo]
balcony/terrace	varanda [va'randa]/terraço [ter'rassoo]
key/room card	chave ['chav-e]/cartão [kar'towng]
luggage/suitcase	bagagem [ba'gazheng]/mala ['mala]/saco ['sakoo]

BANKS, MONEY & CREDIT CARDS

bank/ATM	banco ['bankoo]/multibanco ['multibankoo]
pin code	código pessoal ['kodigoo pesso'al]
cash/ credit card	em dinheiro [eng din'yeyroo]/ com cartão de crédito [kong kar'towng de 'kreditoo]
note/coin	nota ['nota]/moeda [mo'ayda]

HEALTH

doctor/dentist/ paediatrician	médico ['medikoo]/dentista [den'tishta]/ pediatra [pedi'atra]
hospital/ emergency clinic	hospital [oshpi'tal]/ urgências [oor'zhensiash]
fever/pain	febre ['feybre]/dores ['doresh]
diarrhoea/nausea	diarreia [diar'reya]/enjoo [eng'zho]
sunburn	queimadura [keyma'doora]
inflamed/injured	inflamado [infla'madoo]/ferido [fe'ridoo]
plaster/bandage	penso ['pengshoo]/ligadura [liga'doora]
tablet	comprimido [kompri'midoo]

POST, TELECOMMUNICATIONS & MEDIA

stamp/letter/postcard	selo ['seloo]/carta ['karta]/postal [posh'tal]
I'm looking for a prepaid card for my mobile	Procuro um cartão SIM para o meu telemóvel. [pro'kooroo oong kar'towng sim 'para oo meyoo tele'movel]
Where can I find internet access?	Onde há acesso à internet? ['onde a a'ssessoo a 'internet]
computer/battery/ rechargeable battery	computador [kompoota'dor]/pilha ['pilya]/ bateria [bate'ria]
internet connection	ligação à internet [liga'sowng a 'internet]

LEISURE, SPORTS & BEACH

beach/sunshade/ lounger	praia ['praya]/guarda-sol [gwarda 'sol]/ espreguiça-deira [eshpregissa'deyra]
low tide/high tide/ current	maré baixa [ma're 'baisha]/maré alta [ma're alta]/ corrente [kor'rente]

NUMBERS

0	zero ['zeroo]	20	vinte [veengt]
1	um, uma ['oong, 'ooma]	21	vinte e um ['veengt e 'oong]
2	dois, duas ['doysh, 'dooash]	30	trinta ['treengta]
3	três [tresh]	40	quarenta [kwa'renta]
4	quatro ['kwatroo]	50	cinquenta [seeng'kwengta]
5	cinco ['seengkoo]	100	cem ['seng]
6	seis ['seysh]	200	duzentos [doo'zentoosh]
7	sete ['set]	1000	mil ['meel]
8	oito ['oytoo]	2000	dois mil ['doysh meel]
9	nove ['nov]	10.000	dez mil ['desh meel]
10	dez ['desh]	½	um meio ['oong 'meyoo]
11	onze ['ongs]	¼	um quarto [oong 'kwartoo]

STREET ATLAS

The green line indicates the Discovery Tour "Lisbon at a glance"
The blue line indicates the other Discovery Tours
All tours are also marked on the pull-out map

Photo: View over Lisbon

Exploring Lisbon

The map on the back cover shows how the area has been sub-divided

C. da Glória
Av. da Liberdade
R. Condes
Pena
C. N. Colégio
R. M. Vaz
T. da Graça
Rua
A
134
B
Coliseu
Santana
C

Rua António Glória
T. do Fala
Sō
Rua da Glória
R. Portas de Santo Antão
i
L. do Convento da Encarnaç.
R.D.A. da Palma
T. do Tabelião

1
Rua das
Praça dos Restauradores
P
Esc.
R. J. do Regedor
L. São Santana
Garcia

R. São Pedro
S. Pedro
Palácio Foz
i
Restauradores
M
AeroBus
E. d Barroca
T.S. Antão
Teatro D. Maria II.
L. São Domingos
C. do Paço
R. B. Queirós

2
Pedro
R. Teixeira
Elevador da Glória
Eden Teatro
711
759
Estaç. Rossio
ROSSIO
P. Dom João da Câmara
P. Dom João
T.N.S. Domingos
M
Rossio
R. D. Duarte

T. d. Cara
G. Lusitano
Mus. de Arte Sacra Igr. de São Roque
L. D. Cadaval
R. 1° de Dezembro
Praça Dom Pedro IV
Rossio
Pr. da Figueira

T. do Guarda Mor
4
Trindade Coelho
L. do Duque
Carmo
714 12E 15E
737
R. da Betesga

3
T. da Queimada
Rua das Notícias
R. N. da Oliveira
R. da Condessa
R. do Duque
Conv. do Carmo Museu Arqueol.
Rua do Carmo
R. D. de Santa Justa
3673 71 40

T. do Paço da Cidade
R. da Atalaia
R. Diário das
T. J. de Deus
T. da Trindade
R. da Trindade
L. do Carmo
Elevador S. Justa
Rua da
Assun

T. dos F. de Deus
R. Barroca
Teatro Trindade
T. do Carmo
S.S. Sacramento
Rua da
da
Vitor

R. d. Loreto
Espera
Gáveas
P
Salgadeiras
Igr. N.S. da Loreto
Baixa-Chiado
M
Aurea
R. do Ouro
BAIXA

R. das Chagas
R. d. H.
L. d. Camões
R. d. Seca
da
 Igr. N.S. Encarn.
R. Garrett
R. Serpa
C. N. S. Francisco
R. do Crucifixo
Sapateiros
Correeiro

4
Palácio do Manteigueiro
Largo do Barão de Quintela
Rua do Alecrim
R.B.D. de
L. S. Carlos
CHIADO
R. Capelo
Ivens
12
Almada

T. G. Cóussoul
T. do
Teatro S. Luis
R. A° María
Bragança
Pinto
Teatro Nac. S. Carlos
Governo Civil
C. de S. Francisco
Rua da
de

Beco Apóstolos
Emenda
R. Vitor
Museu de Bellas Artes (Mus. do Chiado)
L. d. S. Julião

1 Tv. do Alecrim
R. d. S. Paulo
Ordem Terceira
T. do Ferragial
R. H. Noguera
do
Arco do Au
Min. Admin.

Pr. de São Paulo
R. Remolares
Nov.
Rua do Alecrim
R. C. Santo
R. do Ferragial
Córdon
Pr. do Município
Cam. Munic.
Arsenal
1

D. Amelia
P. D. da Terceira
Carvalho
R. B. Costa
Rua do
ex. Ministério da Marinha
P
Município
i
Welcome Center
Ministério de Agricultura

706;714;728
732;760
M
Cais do Sodré
Corpo Santo
Av. da Ribeira das Naus

Cais do Sodré
P
706 735 736
758 781 782
AeroBus

Estaçao Fluvial Cais do Sodré
134

120

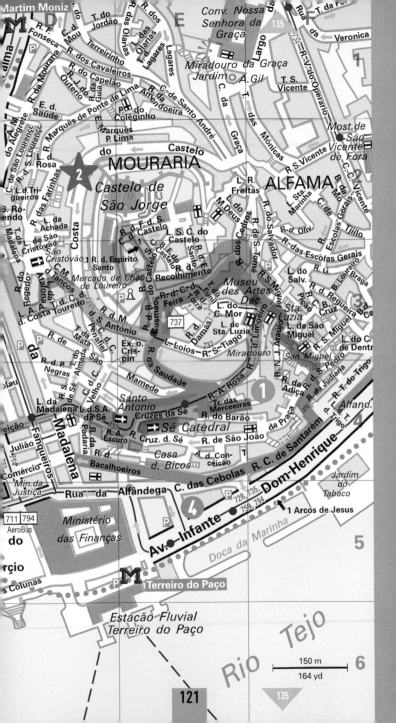

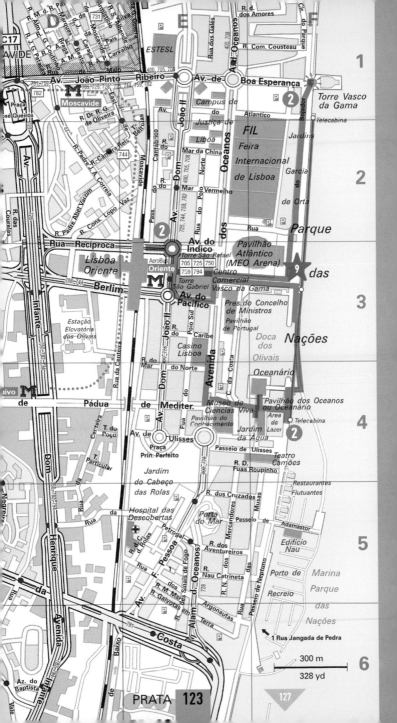

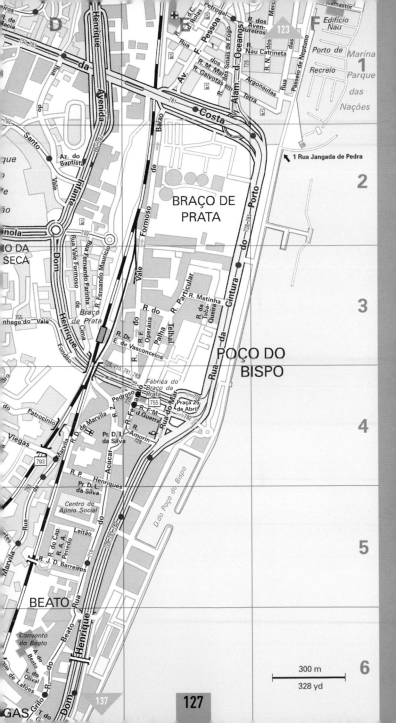

Parque A

Barcal

Espaço
Monsanto

Club de
Tiro
a Chumbo

Ecológico

de Monsanto

B

Benfica

Rua-São

Sitio
do Calhau

C

Rua Francis

Palácio Marquês
de Fronteira

R. A.
Macedo

1

Florestal

de

Monsanto

Estrada

da Serafina

Janeiro

Estrada

de

Parque do
Calhau

**BAIRRO DAS
FURNAS**

Forte de Monsanto

2

Avenida

Monsanto

Martins

Vinte

e

Espaço

Militar

Ministério
de Defesa
Nacional

Tenente

3

Quatro

Serafina

P

da

Parque da Alto da Serafina

Parque
Recreativo

R. Dezoito

R. Catorze

R. D

R. Padre-José G

**ALTO DA
SERAFINA**

Miradouro
do Monsanto

Vista

Bela

Estrada

da

Serafina

4

Auto-estrada IC15 A5 do

Oeste

V.D.-Pacheco

1

Ceuta

Viaduto-Duarte-Pa

Claros

do

5

Florestal

Alvito

Parque Infantil
do Alvito

Estrada

de

da

Monsanto

Ponte

Avenida

R.

300 m

328 yd

6

Estrada

Estrangeira

Club de tenis
de Lisboa

Mentosa d'Baixo

Casal Vist

R. Trest

Tapada

Campo
de Rugby

132

da

**BAIRRO
DO ALVITO**

de

128

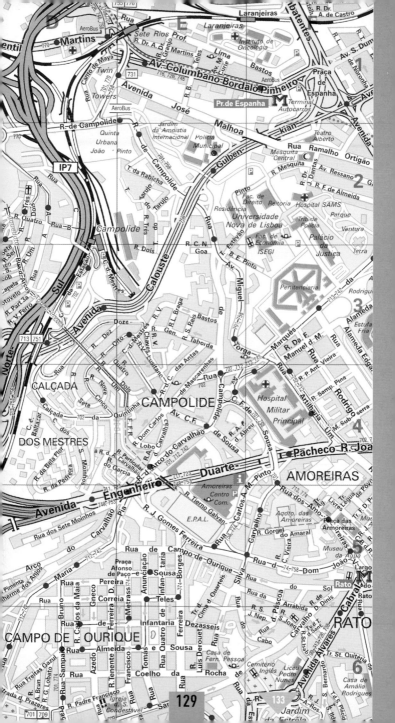

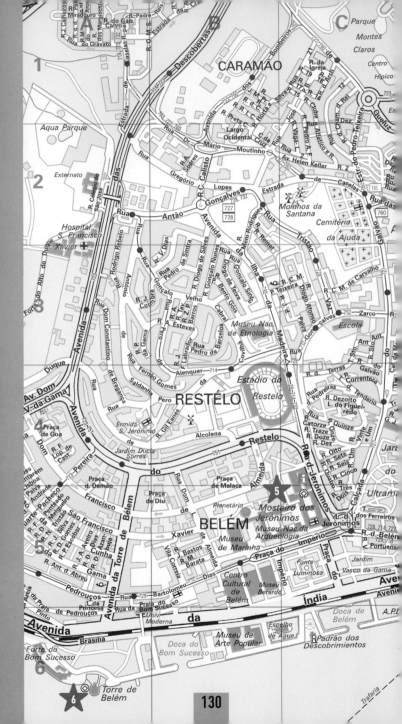

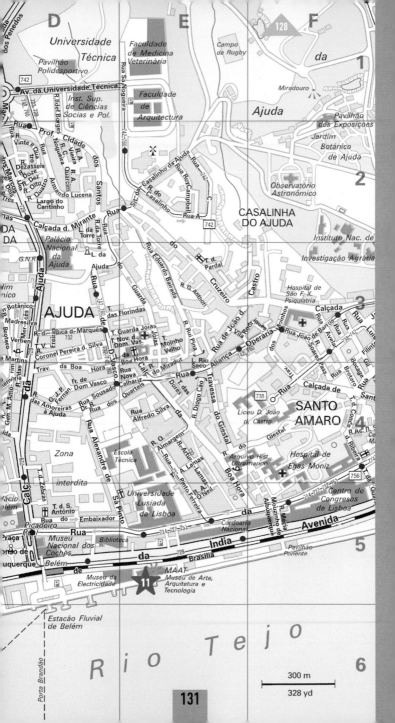

D **E** **F**

Universidade Técnica

Faculdade de Medicina Veterinária

Campo de Rugby

128

da

1

Pavilhão Polidesportivo

Av. da Universidade Técnica

742

Inst. Sup. de Ciências Sociais e Pol.

Faculdade de Arquitectura

Miradouro

Ajuda

Pavilhão des Exposições

Jardim Botânico de Ajuda

2

Prof.

Cidade d.

Rua Sá Nogueira

Largo do Cantinho

Armando Lucena

R. do Casalinho

Rua Roy Campbell

742

Observatório Astronómico

Calçada d. Mirante

L. da Torre

Casalinho da Ajuda

Rua-A

742

CASALINHA DO AJUDA

Instituto Nac. de

Investigação Agrária

3

Palácio Nacional da Ajuda

G.N.R.

L. da Ajuda

Rua da Torre

Rua Eduardo Bairrada

T. d. Pardal

R. G. Anthoni

Cruzeiro

Castro

Hospital de São F. X. Psiquiatria

Calçada

AJUDA

Botânico

Madresilva

Verben

T. das Florindas

Bica-d-Marquesa

732

Coronel Pereira d. Silva

T. Guarda Joias

T. Nov. Dom. Vas.

da Boa Hora

Moinho Velho

Rua de João de Vila

Rua Pina

Operária

Rua João de Barros

Aveiral

R. Brotero

3

Martins

Trav. da Boa Hora

Rua Fernan. Dom Vasco

R. U.P.

das Amoreiras à Ajuda

Fr. te

Rua Sousado

Dr. Rua dos Quarteis

Rua Nova

Calharia

do Miradouro

R. das Dores

Rua

Travessa do Giestal

Rio Seco

Aliança

Trav.

Calçada de

SANTO AMARO

Santo

4

Zona interdita

Escola Técnica

Rua Alfredo Silva

Rua Alexandre de Sá Pinto

R. Q. Almargem

R. Lamas

R. Artur Pinta-Ferreira

A. J. O'Neil

R. Diogo Cão

do Giestal

738

Liceu D. João d. Castro

Arquivo Hist. Ultramarino

R. Boa Hora

Hospital de Egas Moniz

R. Conc. d. Ribeira

R.A.C.

Centro de Congresos de Lisboa

756

744

5

Palácio Belém

T. d. S. António

Rua do Embaixador

Picadeiro

Praça

ção de

uquerque

Museu Nacional dos Coches

Biblioteca

Rua

Belém

da

728

Universidade Lusiada de Lisboa

Cordoaria Nacional

Moizinho de Albuquerque

R. Mec.

Avenida

India

Brasília

Pavilhão Ponente

5

Museu da Electricidade

11

MAAT Museu de Arte, Arquitectura e Tecnologia

Estação Fluvial de Belém

Porta Brandão

Rio Tejo

6

300 m

328 yd

131

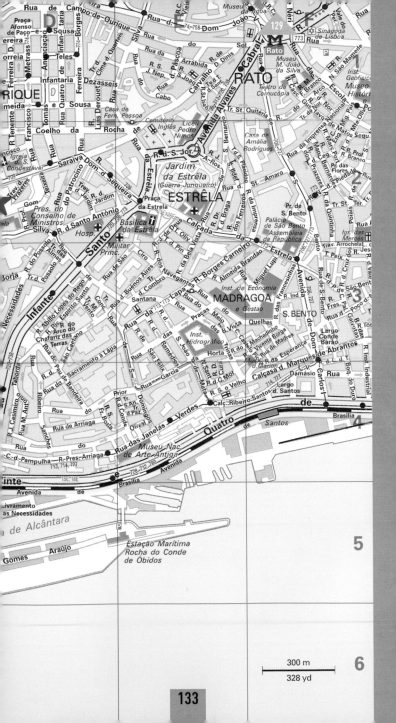

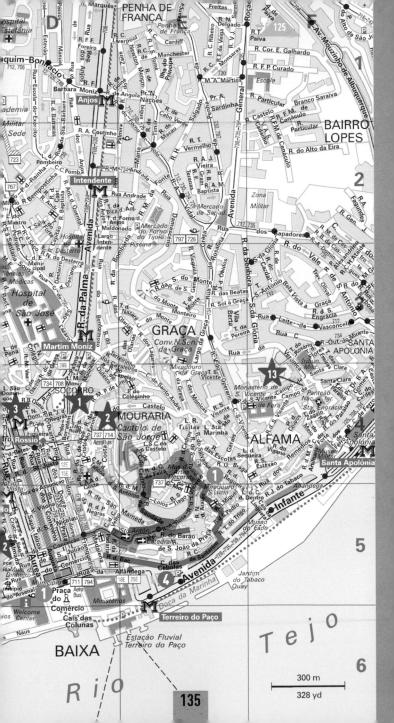

300 m

328 yd

135

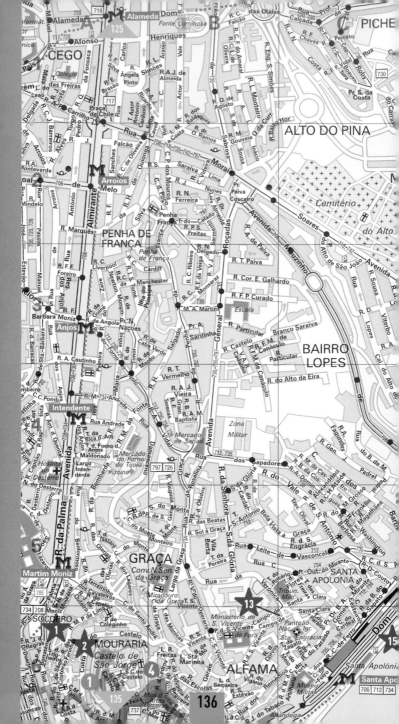

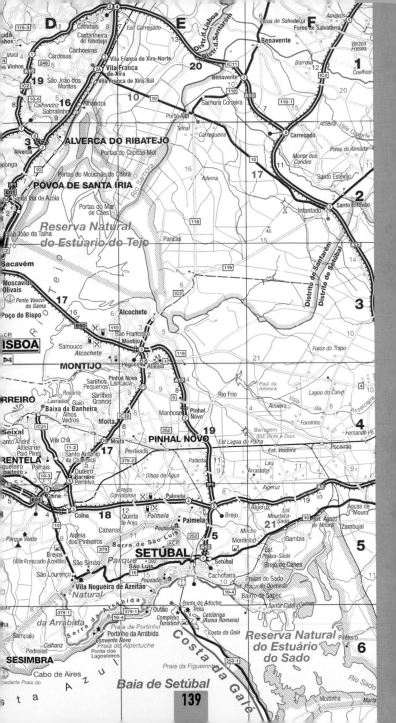

Grid references (top): D, E, F

Column/row markers: 1, 2, 3, 4, 5, 6

Cadafais
Castanheira do Ribatejo
Cachoeiras
Est. Carregado
Foros de Salvaterra
Foros de Salvaterra
Varzea Fresca
Cardosas
Mata
Vinhos
Vila Franca de Xira-Norte
Benavente
Barrosa
Coelhos
São João dos Montes
Vila Franca de Xira
Vila Franca de Xira-Sul
IC11
Benavente
Caihandriz
Sobralinho
Alhandra
Samora Correia
Aroeira Vale Giestro
ALVERCA DO RIBATEJO
Alverca
Portas do Capitão Mór
Porto Alto
Carregueira
Carregado
Monte dos Condes
Foros do Almada
Portas do Mouchão da Cabra
Adema
Santo Estêvão
PÓVOA DE SANTA IRIA
Santa Iria de Azóia
Portas do Mar de Cães
Infantado
Santo Estêvão
Reserva Natural do Estuário do Tejo
São João da Talha
Pancas
Distrito de Santarém
Distrito de Setúbal
Sacavém
Moscavide
Olivais
Ponte Vasco da Gama
Poço do Bispo
Alcochete
Foros do Trapo
LISBOA
São Francisco
Montijo
Samouco
Alcochete
MONTIJO
Pegões
Atalaia
Foros do Trapo
Sarilhos Pequenos
Pinhal Novo
Larcada
Rio Frio
Paúl da Amieira
Lagoa do Calvo
BARREIRO
Rosário
Lavradio
Gaio
Sarilhos Grande
Alhos Vedros
Manhoso
Pinhal Novo
Amieira
Forninho
Fernando Pó
Baixa da Banheira
Moita
IC32
Barragem dos Vinte e Dois
Poceirão
Seixal
Santo André
Aldeia de Paió Pires
Vila Chã
Santo António da Charneca
PINHAL NOVO
Est. Lagoa da Palha
Est. Valdera
Penteado
Palhota
Lau
Arraiados
 quteiro
gueteiro
Palhais
Outeiro Barreiro Penalva
Olhos de Água
Algeruz
Águas de Moura
COINA
Brejos Corrictaira
Palmela
Brejo
Algeruz
Est. Mourisca-Sado
Est. Águas do Moura
Zambujal
Coína
Quinta do Anjo
Palmela
PALMELA
Mocho
Montinho
Gambia
Cabanas
Pousada
Est. Praia-Sado
Brejo de Canes
Aldeia dos Pinheiros
Serra de São Luis
SETÚBAL
Setúbal
Cachofarra
Praias do Sado
Parque Verde
Brejos (Vila Fresco Azeitão)
São Simão
Parque
São Luis
Pousada
Cetóbriga (Ruina Romana)
Bairro de Sapec
Vila Nogueira de Azeitão
Natural
Santa Catalina
Outão
Tróia
Complexo Turístico
da Arrábida
Portinho da Arrábida
Praia de Alpertuche
Costa da Galé
Reserva Natural do Estuário do Sado
Pinheiro
Sampaio
Calhariz
Serra da Arrábida
Convento Novo
Ponta dos Lagosteiros
SESIMBRA
Pedreias
Cabo de Aires
Praia da Figueirinha
Baía de Setúbal
Costa da Galé
Rio Sado
Moitinha
Murta

139

This index lists a selection of the streets and squares shown on the street atlas

STREET INDEX

	Motorway Autobahn
	Road with four lanes Vierspurige Straße
	Thoroughfare - Main road Durchgangsstraße - Hauptstraße
	Other roads Sonstige Straßen
	Information - Parking place Information - Parkplatz
	One-way street - Pedestrian zone Einbahnstraße - Fußgängerzone
	Main railway with station Hauptbahn mit Bahnhof
	Other railway Sonstige Bahn
	Underground, under construction U-Bahn, in Bau
	Tramway - Bus-route Straßenbahn - Buslinie
	Shipping route - Cableway Schifffahrtslinie - Standseilbahn
	Church of interest - Other church Sehenswerte Kirche - Sonstige Kirche
	Mosque - Synagogue Moschee - Synagoge
	Post office - Monument - Windmill Postamt - Denkmal - Windmühle
	Hospital - Youth hostel - Camping site Krankenhaus - Jugendherberge - Campingplatz
	Built-up area, public building Bebaute Fläche, öffentliches Gebäude
	Park, forest - Cemetery Park, Wald - Friedhof
	Industrial area - Municipal boundary Industriegelände - Stadtgrenze
	MARCO POLO Discovery Tour 1 MARCO POLO Erlebnistour 1
	MARCO POLO Discovery Tours MARCO POLO Erlebnistouren
	MARCO POLO Highlight MARCO POLO Highlight

MARCO POLO TRAVEL GUIDES

Travel with
Insider
Tips

INDEX

This index lists all sights and destinations plus the main squares, streets, names and key terms featured in this guide. Numbers in bold indicate a main entry.

CREDITS

WRITE TO US

e-mail: info@marcopologuides.co.uk

Did you have a great holiday?
Is there something on your mind?
Whatever it is, let us know!
Whether you want to praise, alert us to errors or give us a personal tip – MARCO POLO would be pleased to hear from you.
We do everything we can to provide the very latest information for your trip.

Nevertheless, despite all of our authors' thorough research, errors can creep in. MARCO POLO does not accept any liability for this. Please contact us by e-mail or post.

MARCO POLO Travel Publishing Ltd
Pinewood, Chineham Business Park
Crockford Lane, Chineham
Basingstoke, Hampshire RG24 8AL
United Kingdom

PICTURE CREDITS
Cover Photograph: Torre de Belém (Look: H. Leue)
Photographs: R. Freyer (71); Getty Images/Volvo Ocean Race: I. Roman (50); Getty Images/EyeEm: G. Bakos (103); huber-images: S. Lubenow (14/15, 72), M. Pavan (26/27); huber-images/SIME: J. Huber (32/33); G. Knoll (35); laif: T. Gerber (36, 40, 58, 66/67, 106 bottom, 107), M. Gonzalez (63), A. Hub (105), H. Meyer (89), T. & R. Morandi (6, 49), F. Siemers (4 bottom, 56/57, 74/75); laif/ASEE: L. F. Catarino (42, 78); laif/GAMMA-RAPHO: A. Toureau (18 top); laif/hemis.fr: F. Guiziou (22), J. Heintz (18 bottom), P. Jacques (7, 45), S. Torrione (104), M. Zublena (84); laif/robertharding: R. Moiola (flap right); laif/SZ Photo: J. Giribas (65, 81); Look: J. Greune (4 top, 17, 19 bottom), K. Johaentges (53, 61), H. Leue (1, 104/105); Look/age fotostock (118/119); Look/SagaPhoto (76); mauritius images/age (102/103); mauritius images/Alamy (2, 8, 9, 10, 30, 101, 102), P. Bernhardt (87), M. Gottschalk (flap left, 106 top), I. Musto (82/83), K. Welsh (46); mauritius images/Endless Travel/Alamy (19 top); mauritius images/foodcollection (62 left, 62 right); mauritius images/Hemis.fr: P. Jacques (54, 90/91); mauritius images/Imagebroker: E. Bömsch (95), S. Kiefer (68), S. Kuttig (5), J. Piqozne (39), M. Wolf (12/13); mauritius images/robertharding: G&M Therin-Weise (20/21); mauritius images/Rubberball (3); mauritius images/Westend61: Z. Dangubic (18 centre); mauritius images/Zoonar/Alamy (25); T. Stankiewicz (11)

3rd Edition – fully revised and updated 2020
Worldwide Distribution: Marco Polo Travel Publishing Ltd, Pinewood, Chineham Business Park, Crockford Lane, Basingstoke, Hampshire RG24 8AL, United Kingdom. Email: sales@marcopolouk.com
© MAIRDUMONT GmbH & Co. KG, Ostfildern
Chief editor: Stefanie Penck; Author: Annette Hüller, co-author: Kathleen Becker, Editor: Petra Klose
Programme supervision: Lucas Forst-Gill, Susanne Heimburger, Johanna Jiranek, Nikolai Michaelis, Kristin Wittemann, Tim Wohlbold; Picture editor: Gabriele Forst, Stefanie Wiese
Cartography street atlas: © MAIRDUMONT, Ostfildern; Cartography pull-out map: © MAIRDUMONT, Ostfildern
Design front cover, p. 1, pull-out map cover: Karl Anders – Büro für Visual Stories, Hamburg; interior: milchhof:atelier, Berlin; Discovery Tours, p. 2/3: Susan Chaaban Dipl.-Des. (FH).
Translated by Susan Jones, Tübingen; Prepress: writehouse, Cologne
Phrase book in cooperation with Ernst Klett Sprachen GmbH, Stuttgart, Editorial by Pons Wörterbücher

MIX
Paper from responsible sources
FSC® C124385

DOS & DON'TS ✊

DON'T BE PUSHY

On the bus and tram, things are very British: passengers take their place in the queue. And if you don't want to risk a fit on the part of the driver, don't ever board a bus at the back!

DON'T SAY "GRACIAS" FOR THANK YOU

"Thank you" in Portuguese is *obrigada* (from a lady) and *obrigado* (from a gentleman). If you don't want to out yourself as an arrogant foreigner, don't use the Spanish *gracias*.

DON'T BECOME CARELESS

Lissabon is casual. But still: a wallet in your back pocket, an iPhone on the café table or valuables at the very top inside your bag are an invitation to thieves. When strolling through dark old town lanes, don't carry a lot of cash with you or flash your camera or phone too openly. Women are not chatted up as much as in other southern countries, but they should take the usual precautions.

DON'T WANDER DARK STREETS ALONE AT NIGHT

Around the party mile of Bairro Alto and in Alfama in particular, avoid lonely lanes at night. Lisbon might be Europe's second-safest capital, but muggings do occur! If in doubt, take a taxi (they are cheap!)

DON'T SLAG OFF PORTUGAL

In these difficult times of austerity measures, calling Portugal "a Third World country" or "an embarrassment" is the prerogative of the locals...

DON'T TURN UP TOO EARLY

The Portuguese sense of time could be called "elastic". If invited to dinner, turning up on the dot risks embarrassing your hosts. Fifteen minutes after the agreed time is a safe bet. This applies to both parties of course.

DON'T BUY LAURELS INSTEAD OF CANNABIS

In tolerant Portugal, owning mini portions of cannabis for personal use is legal. Tricky dealers sometimes exploit clueless tourists by selling them (especially in the Baixa) pressed laurel. An expensive treat – without any High...

DON'T JUST EAT

Bread, cheese, olives and ham are already on your restaurant table? Nice, but these delicacies, the *couvert*, can become expensive. According to law *(Lei do Couvert*, 2015*)*, guests don't have to pay for anything they haven't ordered or consumed. In any case, the price of these things has to be shown on the menu or told to the customer. It's best to return everything you don't want immediately; if in doubt, ask! And check the bill carefully after your meal.